He Came Preaching
PEACE

CALL TO PEACEMAKING

The New Call to Peacemaking (which took the initiative in preparing *He Came Preaching Peace* for publication) is a cooperative program of Brethren, Friends, and Mennonites with the purpose of strengthening peace convictions and actions within their own ranks and searching with other Christians for a faithful response in the world today to the call of Jesus to love and nonviolence. New Call to Peacemaking, Edgar Metzler, National Coordinator, Box 1245, Elkhart, IN 46515.

He Came
Preaching
PEACE

Sponsored by the New Call to Peacemaking

John H. Yoder

Foreword by
Vernon Grounds

A Christian Peace Shelf Selection

HERALD PRESS
Scottdale, Pennsylvania
Kitchener, Ontario
1985

Library of Congress Cataloging in Publication Data

Yoder, John Howard.
  He came preaching peace.

  "Sponsored by the New Call to Peacemaking."
  "A Christian peace shelf selection."
  Bibliography: p.
  1. Peace—Biblical teaching. 2. Bible—Criticism,
interpretation, etc. I. Title.
BS680.P4Y63 1985   261.8'73   85-5474
ISBN 0-8361-3395-1 (pbk. : alk. paper)

The biblical translations used in this book are often adapted by the author
in the interest of style or accuracy, drawing on several of the newer versions.
A specific source is indicated only when the citation is verbatim or nearly so.

HE CAME PREACHING PEACE
Copyright © 1985 by Herald Press, Scottdale, Pa. 15683
  Published simultaneously in Canada by Herald Press,
  Kitchener, Ont. N2G 4M5
Library of Congress Catalog Card Number: 85-5474
International Standard Book Number: 0-8361-3395-1
Printed in the United States of America
Design by Alice B. Shetler

90 89 88 87 86 85 10 9 8 7 6 5 4 3 2 1

Dedicated to the memory of
H. S. Bender and Orie O. Miller,
whose respective committees
in the summer of 1948
first assigned me the
task of church peace
education;

to Elmer Neufeld,
who administered the summer
"peace team" circuit;

and to
John A. Hostetler
and Willard Hunsberger,
who shared in that freshman ministry.

Contents

Foreword

The common sin of a book reviewer is to indulge in high-flown eulogy. To do so is indeed a sin; it makes a mockery of critical intelligence and even simple honesty. Unless the eulogy is deserved! Then truth requires, if not unqualified eulogy, at least sincere praise. In my opinion, John Howard Yoder has given us one of those rare books which merit enthusiastic endorsement.

Why camouflage my admiration for this Mennonite champion of biblical peacemaking? Through the years I, moving in a different ecclesiastical tradition, have found Yoder's writings a source of provocative insight. More persuasively than perhaps any other contemporary, he has been an eloquent advocate of God's *shalom*.

Ironically, dialoguing with such theological giants as Karl Barth and Reinhold Niebuhr, he has pointed out their inconsistencies while maintaining against them an unfaltering and convincing witness to the antiviolent, cross-bearing discipleship demanded by our Lord.

Yoder's creative reinterpretation of New Testament ethics, *The Politics of Jesus*, was and remains a landmark study. His recent discussions, *What Would You Do?* and *When War Is Unjust*, help to clarify some of the issues which trouble obedient citizens of *The Priestly Kingdom*, as he has entitled still another of his newer publications. Pervading all his writing, as it does his thinking and living, is a passion for justice, freedom, and peace under the kingship of Jesus Christ.

Here, then, helpfully gathered together into a single volume, is the rich harvest of Yoder's lifelong probing of Scripture. This book is an invaluable resource for all of us who prayerfully wrestle with the inspired text, attempting to fathom and flesh out what it teaches concerning that multifaceted peace which reflects the God of peace incarnate in the Prince of Peace.

Vernon Grounds
President Emeritus, Denver Conservative
   Baptist Seminary
President, Evangelicals for Social Action

Author's Preface

He came and preached peace to you who were far off
and peace to those who were near.
Ephesians 2:17

What this biblical text originally meant was not that Jesus was a preacher in any ordinary sense of the word. It does not refer to his verbal ministry. Rather, it says that his life and death incarnated a message—that his total being in the world heralded the new state of things which it describes as "peace."

Nonetheless, we are not presumptuous or confused when we attempt to reflect upon that enfleshed proclamation in words of our own. This confession is laid upon us as a duty, if we hold the events it reflects to be true.

When the text names "those who are near," we are reminded of the fact that a large part of the communication going on within any committed human group is not an effort to inform or convince outsiders, but a process of renewing and of deepening the understanding or the decision of those already sharing in the body. The chapters in this book were all originally addressed orally by a believer to believers. Just as Jesus brought to his own people nothing which was not already their own, just as the apostle Paul's proclamation of the opening of Israel to the Gentiles is a message only a Jew could address only to Jews, so these meditations are without apology "peace church" in-group communication.

The actual ministry of the apostle, in fact, was mostly to "those who were near." It was those who were already participating in the believing heritage who most needed to be addressed.

The messages on the pages which follow are not argument to outsiders (neither apology nor evangelism to the Gentiles). They are addressed to persons already engaged in the Christian peace movement, as a contribution toward making more coherent their already growing conviction. Yet neither is this material catechism. It walks in a celebrative mood through the major themes of our Scriptures, without using any checklists or standard formulas to be sure nothing has been missed.

The commonality of these studies lies on the broadest level of theme and orientation. They are not the same in their style, nor in the kind of text being studied, nor in the way of developing it. The cross-reference to active national and institutional peacemaking is intentionally indirect, although constantly just below the surface. The several texts interpreted all speak of the people of God present in the midst of the world yet not identified with it—responsible yet not in charge. They tend deliberately to be talking more about the place of the people of God in the history of the world under God than of individual spirituality—although that distinction would become thinner with closer attention.

The chapters in this book might be spoken of by some as "sermons." They are addressed to believers, assuming the readiness of readers or listeners to be exhorted and instructed. Yet they were not prepared or presented in a context of congregational worship. They lack some of those elements of illustration and rhetoric that normally have a place in the "sermon."

The genre of the "Bible lecture" has a long and worthy, if now largely forgotten, history in the evangelical experience. Its straightforward style, its direct attention to the text, its length presuppose the place which the Bible as education had in the Puritan church, the Restoration movement, and the frontier college.

The Bible lecture filled a particular place in the church life of frontier America. It was a pattern of educational communication that assumed on the part of many members a wide base of literacy and a high level of responsible involvement in the life of the church. A Bible lecturer would come to a local church anywhere in the Midwest, anytime from 1850 to 1930, with the solid expectation that he would find a committed body of serious listeners ready to come to meetings every evening for a week or two. They would follow his textual exposition in their well-worn Bibles. While open to accepting from the lecturer any level of erudition and special information about language or archeology or ancient Near Eastern cultural contexts, they believed that it is the business of every lay Christian to listen critically and to "look in the texts themselves to know whether it was as they said" (the pattern of the Jews in Berea, Acts 17:11).

Mennonites, Brethren, Friends, Disciples (the peace churches of the American frontier) maintained for a few generations, in a costly and critical way, that special vision of a literate lay biblical culture, independent of the services of specialized clergy, yet respectful of the ministry of scholarship. A century later it is a privilege to share in the initiative of the New Call to Peacemaking, as it reenacts the heritage of frontier biblical renewal in the modest yet presumptuous, risky yet confident exercise of going back to the Scripture together.

The first presentation of the lectures in this book was spread across an entire generation. Some were given more than once, in differing forms. There has been little attempt to purge the texts of the marks of their original contexts, allowing the reader to make the obvious current applications.

That the peace of Christ should be a theme of proclamation stands in contradiction to the perennial preoccupation of some strands of Christianity to distinguish between divine and human revelation, between the spiritual and the social gospel, between mind and body, or between inward and outward reconciliation. That dualistic theme is seldom debated in this book in an explicit way, but is constantly under attack by assumption and by implication. It is not simply that the theologian has an obligation to maintain intellectual balance by giving similar weights to both sides of a dialectic. It is rather that the person of Jesus rises above such dichotomies and empowers his disciples to do the same.

It is first of all the person of Jesus who proclaimed the peace from which this book has taken its title. It is his glory and his vulnerability that negate the dichotomy, and it is to the power of that glory and that transcendance that this modest offering is dedicated and entrusted.

John H. Yoder
Elkhart, Indiana
March 26, 1984

He Came Preaching
PEACE

1

The Way of Peace in a
World at War

I. Portraits of Christ

Following the example of Jesus himself, the first Christians and the writers of the New Testament were quick to see in the book of the prophet Isaiah a description of the innocent sufferings of Christ. They read there:

> He was counted among evildoers. . . .
> For our welfare he was chastised. . . .
> Mistreated, he bore it humbly, without complaint,
> silent as a sheep led to the slaughter,
> silent as a ewe before the shearers. . . .
> They did away with him unjustly. . . .
> though he was guilty of no violence
> and had not spoken one false word.
>
> *Isaiah 53:4-9*

In all ages these words of the prophet concerning the one he called the "Servant of the Lord" have been beloved by Christians for the portrait they paint of our crucified Master. Yet when we find these same words echoing in the New Testament, it is not only because they are fitting or beautiful words to describe Christ and his sacrifice on behalf of sinful humanity; it is because they constitute a call to the Christian to do likewise. There we read:

> If you have done right and suffer for it
> your endurance is worthwhile in the sight of God;
> To this you were called,
> because Christ suffered on your behalf,
> and left you an example;
> it is for you to follow in his steps,
> He committed no sin,
> he was guilty of no falsehood;
> when he suffered he uttered no threats.

1 Peter 2:20-22

The innocent, silently uncomplaining suffering of Christ is, in the teaching of Peter, whose letter I have just quoted, not only an act of Christ on our behalf from which we benefit; it is also an example of Christ for our instruction, which we are to follow. This portrait of Christ is to be painted again on the ordinary canvas of our lives. Did not Jesus himself say that those who would follow him must deny themselves and take up their cross? What then does it mean for the Christian to bear a cross?

What Is Our Cross?

We meet in this world some suffering that is our own fault; we bring accidents upon ourselves by our carelessness, or punishment by our own offenses. This is not "bearing a cross." As Peter wrote, there is no merit in taking punishment for having done wrong. "What credit is it," he asks, "if when you do wrong and are beaten for it, you take it patiently?"

We also sometimes suffer in ways we cannot understand, as from an unexpected or unexplained illness or catastrophe. Such suffering the Christian can bear, trusting in God's supporting presence and learning to depend more fully and more joyfully on him. Yet this is not what Jesus was talking about when he predicted suffering for his disciples.

The cross of Christ was the price of his obedience to God amidst a rebellious world; it was suffering for having done right, for loving where others hated, for representing in the flesh the forgiveness and the righteousness of God among men both less forgiving and less righteous. The cross of Christ was God's method of overcoming evil with good.

The cross of the Christian is no different. It is the price of one's obedience to God's love toward all people in a world ruled by hate. Such unflinching love for friend and foe alike will mean hostility and suffering for us, as it did for him.

Jesus instructed his disciples, simply and clearly, not to resist evil.

> Whoever slaps you on the right cheek, turn and offer him the left. If he sues you for your shirt, let him have your coat as well. . . . Love your enemies and pray for those who persecute you, only so can you be the children of your heavenly Father who sends his sun and rain to good and bad alike.
>
> *Matthew 5:39-45*

In saying this, Jesus was not a foolish dreamer spinning out futile hopes for a better world, thinking that if only we keep smiling everything will turn out all right, with our opponents turned into friends and our sacrifices all repaid. He knew full well the cost of such unlimited love. He foresaw clearly the suffering it would mean, first for himself and then for his followers. But there was no other way for him to take, no other way worthy of God. Jesus' teaching here is not a collection of good human ideas; it is his divinely authoritative interpretation of the law of God.

Facing Our Conflicts

Over the years the world has not grown much more loving. The example of Cain, who killed his brother, still sets the basic pattern for dealing with conflicts, whether within the family or in the world of nations. Among nations it matters little whether they profess to be religious or not. The choice of weapons and the readiness to retaliate are similar. How few are they, how few even within the Christian churches, who in this embattled world seek to be conformed only to Christ, to find in the suffering servant of the Lord, and not in some honored king or warrior, the model for their lives!

"It is by this that we know what love is," says the apostle, "that Christ laid down his life for us. And we in turn are bound to lay down our lives for our brothers" (1 John 3:16, NEB).

Christians whose loyalty to the Prince of Peace puts them out of step with today's nationalistic world, because they are willing to love their nation's friends but not to hate their nation's enemies, are not unrealistic dreamers who think that by their objections they will end all wars. On the contrary, it is the soldiers who think they can put an end to wars by preparing for just one more. Nor do such Christians think that by virtue of their refusal to help with the organized destruction of life and property they are uninvolved in the complications and conflicts of modern life. Nor are they reacting in emotional fear to the fantastic awfulness of the weapons created by the demonic ingenuity of modern scientists.

They love their enemies not because they think they are wonderful people, not because they think their love is sure to conquer them, not because they fail to respect their native land or their rulers, not because they are unconcerned for the safety of their neighbors, not because they favor another political or economic system.

Christians love their enemies because God does so, and commands his followers to do so. That is the only reason, and that is enough. Our God, who has made himself known in Jesus Christ, is a reconciling, a forgiving, a suffering God. If, to paraphrase the apostle Paul, "it is no longer I who love, but Christ who loves in me" (Galatians 2:20), my life must bear the marks of that revelation.

We Have No Enemies

No one created in God's image and for whom Christ died can be for me an enemy, whose life I am willing to threaten or to take, unless I am more devoted to something else—to a political theory, to a nation, to the defense of certain privileges, or to my own personal welfare—than I am to God's cause: his loving invasion of this world in his prophets, his Son, and his church.

One of the most difficult things to understand in the history of the Christian church is the haste with which preachers and simple citizens have labeled the selfish interests of their own class, their own race, their own nation with the name of Christ, making a holy cause of the subjection, or even the destruction, of those whom Christ came to save and to give an abundant life.

In any kind of conflict, from the fist fight to the labor dispute, from the family quarrel to the threat of international communism, the Christian sees the world and its wars from the viewpoint of the cross. "When we were God's enemies, we were reconciled to him through the death of his Son" (Romans 5:10, NEB).

The Christian has no choice. If this was God's pattern, if his strategy for dealing with his enemies was to love them and give himself for them, it must be ours as well.

II. Nationality? Christian

From the top of the mountains I see him;
From the hills I behold him
Lo, a people dwelling alone
and not reckoning itself among the nations.

Numbers 23:9

You are a chosen race,
a royal priesthood,
a holy nation,
God's own people.   *1 Peter 2:9*

It has always been true that people have many loyalties, many attachments to groups or causes for which they are willing to sacrifice. Such loyalty may be to a family or a school, a sporting club, or a business firm. Yet the overwhelming loyalty of most persons in our age is to the nation. Whether under the long-established governments of Europe and North America, or in those other parts of the world where national independence is a recent attainment or a goal still sought after, it is to the nation that young persons give their enthusiasm. For the nation young people will risk their lives. For the nation they will, if need be, kill and destroy in war.

What does Christ say about the Christian and national loyalty? For centuries, most professing Christians have believed that their faith made them not only more obedient citizens but also more courageous soldiers, that God helped them not only to love their neightbors but also to hate and destroy their enemies. Since the Roman emperor Constantine allied his government with the church, priests and preachers have been crowning kings, blessing armies, and praying for the defeat of their nation's enemies, all in the name of the Prince of Peace. Almost every theology and every denomination has explained how this had to be so. Today churchmen can be found who will argue that even the hydrogen bomb, even poison gas or germ warfare, can be used by Christians against their fellowhumans if only the nation so commands. But what does the gospel say?

"Out of Every Nation"

The Bible does not ignore the existence of nations. Once the missionary Paul, addressing a group of philosophers, spoke of how the Creator God had "made from one every nation of people to live on all the face of the earth, having determined allotted periods and the boundaries of their habitation" (Acts 17:26). But most often when we read in Scripture of "the nations," it is to say that *out* of every tribe and tongue and people and *nation* individuals have been redeemed to belong to God's people.

"You are a chosen race, a royal priesthood, a holy *nation*, God's own people," Peter wrote of the Christian church. The nation to which the Christian belongs *first* is "God's own people," the fellowship of the saints, the church of Jesus Christ. This "people for God's special possession" is united not by a common language or territory or government but by one and the same divine call and a common response. Reconciled to God, men and women belong to each other. The unity thus created breaches every wall and rends every curtain, whether of bamboo or of iron.

Then the apostle said that in Christ God had joined "Greek and Jew . . . barbarian, Scythian, whether slave or free" (Colossians 3:11). Today he would say, "white and black, Russian and American, labor and management."

This new nation, the people of God, is the Christian's first loyalty. No political nation, no geographical homeland to which one belongs by birth, can take precedence over the heavenly citizenship of a Christian in one's new birth.

These pious phrases—citizenship in heaven, new birth, people of God—are nothing new. They are in fact so familiar, so well worn, that it occurs to few Christians to stop and think what it would really mean to take them seriously. Well, what would it mean?

Brothers and Sisters in All Nations

First of all, God's call to put first loyalties first means that Christians of different nations, even of enemy nations, have more in common with each other, belong more closely to each other, should care more for each other's welfare than for that of their non-christian fellow citizens. Not for nothing do Christians call one another "brother" or "sister." How then can Christians, for the sake of their country's prestige or possessions, seek to take the lives of their spiritual brothers and sisters, when their sole offense is to have been born under another flag?

Today a great wave of concern for their dividedness is sweeping through the Christian churches. Differences of creed and denominational barriers are felt to be an offense against our Lord's will that his followers should be one as he and his Father are one. Church leaders labor over creeds and put forth considerable effort to be able to worship together. Yet is it not a yet more flagrant betrayal of Christian unity when children of the same Father, disciples of the same Lord, at a word from their secular rulers take up arms against one another?

To confess belief in the church universal means that we cannot grasp all of God's will by keeping our minds tidily fenced within our own borders. For instance, when the apostle Paul instructs his readers to be subject to the powers established over them (Romans 13:1), we cannot conclude, as do so many Christians, that this applies only to us and to our government. Paul wrote this about the rule of pagan Rome. He does not say that freedom-loving people shall be subject only to democratic governments, but that "every soul" shall be subject to the established rulers. If this is the Christian's duty in North America, it is as much the duty of Christians in China or France, in Poland or India.

Our governments may feel that they have reasons to refuse to recognize the existence of certain hostile powers, and even to seek their downfall. Some Christians make a virtue of advocating a more belligerent national policy than their government exercises. Some even consider it impossible that a Christian could live under a fascist or communist government without rebelling. Thereby they admit their lack of understanding of the universality of the church, which through most of history has thrived under unchristian, even tyrannical, governments, and has stagnated when it became the spiritual sponsor of a nation's aims.

Ultimate Values

Finally, the primacy of Christians' loyalty will show in our sense of ultimate values. In the minds of many serious people, what really matters about human history is the creation of institutions which will create and distribute material abundance, and will guarantee human rights. This is what we read about in the history books. These things do matter. And generally Christians do much to help achieve them. But what matters most, the real reason that God lets time go on, is his calling together of his own people through the witness of the gospel. Not building and protecting a bigger and better democracy, but building the church is God's purpose; not the defeat of communism, or of hunger, but the proclamation of his kingdom and the welding of all kinds of men and women into one new body is what we are here for. Kings and empires have come and gone in times past and shall continue to come and go until the day of Christ's appearing. For Christians to seek any government's interest—even the security and power of peaceable and freedom-loving democracy—at the cost of the lives and security of our brothers and sisters around the world, would be selfishness and idolatry, however much glorified by patriotic preachers and poets.

Not only in Abraham's time was it a testing of faith to be called by God to abandon all else out of loyalty to that "city whose builder and maker is God" (Hebrews 11:10). Even more today, when nationalism has become a religion for millions, will the true depth and reality of the Christian profession of church people be tested when they must choose between their earthly and their eternal loyalties.

What is our allegiance? It is to that people "elect from every nation, yet one o'er all the earth." Our nationality? Christian.

III. Disarmed by God

What causes conflicts and quarrels among you? Do they not
spring from the aggressiveness of your bodily desires?
You want something which you cannot have
and so you are bent on murder;
you are envious, and cannot attain your ambition,
and so you quarrel and fight.

James 4:1-2, NEB

These words of the apostle James have not been worn out. When there is conflict, whether within small groups or between nations, we try to dignify the clash with lofty principles. We may speak of truth and honor, of democracy and of human rights, of great causes and of noble goals. Yet the apostle is not deceived: "What is the cause of conflicts among you? . . . is it not your bodily desires? . . . you are envious."

He has seen deeper than we care to admit. True enough, anyone—even groups of people, and perhaps, rarely, a nation— can seek sincerely some unselfish purpose, but only seldom and not for long. If great, noble, unselfish causes are constantly proclaimed as the guides of a group's actions, even the most gullible of us has learned to check a second time to see what the real reason is. In international affairs a nation may show great concern, as they usually say, to "liberate" some poor people from "tyranny." What they really care about, however, is the price of sugar or the use of some mine or port, or the aggrandizement of their political influence. In the dealings between labor and management, each side speaks of the good of the national economy. But the real desire is for an immediate one-sided gain, even at the cost of a rise in prices for everyone. In a neighborhood or family disagreement, we hastily announce that serious moral principles are at stake—honesty or decency—when in fact, it is our own pride that drives us.

Understanding the Cause

If we thus understand the true root of conflict, this explains a number of things. It explains, first of all, *why* the Christian is and must be a child of peace. The Christian is not primarily someone who has joined a church, or has accepted certain teachings, or has had certain feelings, or has promised to live up to certain moral standards, though all these things are part of the picture. The Christian is a person who has been, in the words of Jesus, "born anew," who has started life over, who by the power of God is a new person. Conflict was previously a normal, built-in part of one's nature, but now the person has been disarmed. The spring from which flowed enmity and strife has been clogged. The scrawny shrub of bitterness has been cut down to the stump. It may well spring up again, but the believer knows how to deal with it as with any other temptation—in repentance, confession, and spiritual victory.

The reason, therefore, for the Christian's being called to live above this world's battles is not that one of the Ten Commandments enjoins us not to kill, and not even that Jesus as a new law-giver orders us to love our enemies. The Christian has been disarmed by God. No *orders* are needed to love one's neighbors, beginning in the smallest circle of daily relationships, or with one's enemies. The believer is driven to this by the love of Christ within.

The fact that selfish desire is the root of conflict explains why we cannot really expect whole nations and societies to build a peaceful world. Christian behavior flows from faith; we cannot impose it on entire nations. Many persons, when they hear of

Christians whose conscience forbids their bearing arms, will argue against this position on the grounds that it is quite unrealistic to expect nations to follow this example. This is a strange argument. In our teachings about moral purity and holiness in any other realm, we do not wait for the world to be ready to follow us before we follow Christ. We know clearly that to be called by Christ means being different from the world.

How then should our living the disarmed life depend on whether nations are ready to lay down their weapons? Jesus predicted that there would continue to be wars as long as this world lasts, just as he predicted that people's faith would grow cold and their morals loose. But this cannot be a reason for Christians to follow this world's ways, anymore than the prevalence of theft or of waste is a model for Christians to follow.

Pray for Rulers

When we say that we do not expect nations to take the path of suffering and discipleship, this does not mean that it is wrong for Christians to desire and to work for peace among nations. The apostle Paul expressly instructs us to pray especially for rulers and for all those in authority, in order that we may lead a peaceful life. God's will is that we should be able to live quiet and godly lives. The duty of government before God is to permit this. We therefore can and should pray and testify concerning the folly of trusting in earthly arms, concerning the undermining of democratic government by peacetime military establishment, concerning the dangers of radioactive contamination and of "accidental war" which the great belligerent powers impose on the rest of the globe, and especially concerning the hideous immorality of the weapons now being devised.

It might even be that with more and more of our neighbors uneasy and disturbed about the menace of militarism, the example and refusal of a few resolute Christians could sound an alarm, a rallying cry for intelligent citizens who were waiting for someone with the courage to speak first and to suffer for it. But the Christian does not renounce war because one can expect intelligent citizens to rally around. They usually won't. The believer takes that stand because the defenseless death of the Messiah has for all time been revealed as the victory of faith that overcomes the world.

But wait a minute. Is this the whole picture? Is there not, after all, a moral difference between freedom and tyranny? Is it not our duty to care and even to sacrifice for the preservation of our civilization? Certainly not all such sacrifice can be accounted for as "selfish desires." Are we not socially responsible? The Christian who has been disarmed by God has several things to say at this point, but they may be gathered up into one question. Did not Jesus Christ face the same problem? Was not he, who was just as human as you and I, concerned for the victims of oppression? Was he not, with the thousands who gathered around to make him king, a man before whom the path to political responsibility was opening? Did he not believe that it was God's prophetically announced will to glorify himself by establishing righteousness among the nations and to make Zion the center from which justice would go out to all peoples?

The Supreme Example

And yet all of this did not swerve the Son of Man, in whom we see what God wants each of us to be, from his certainty that to seek and to save the lost his path must be one not of power but of humility—not of enforcing justice but of incarnating love. As Peter wrote, "He . . . committed his cause to the One who judges justly" (1 Peter 2:23, NEB). Yet has not the ministry of this one defenseless man—and of the line of disarmed martyrs in his train across the years—done more to unseat tyrants and to defend basic human rights than all the belligerent zeal of those who were seeking to defend God's people against the godless with the weapons of war? Human wrath does not accomplish the justice of God.

When the apostle Paul says that "the weapons we wield are not merely human" or "not those of the world" (2 Corinthians 10:4, NEB), most of us, accustomed to thinking on the "merely human" level, would have expected him to say, "not human but spiritual," or, "not of this world but of the other world." But he says, "not merely human, but divinely potent." This is the "almighty meekness" of our reigning Lord. When the Christian whom God has disarmed lays aside carnal weapons it is not, in the last analysis, because those weapons are too strong, but because they are too weak. He directs his life toward the day when all creation will praise not kings and chancellors but the Lamb that was slain as worthy to receive blessing and honor and glory *and power* (Revelation 5:12-13).

First presented as three broadcast talks on *The Mennonite Hour*, 1968. Later printed in *Sojourners* and in *El Discipulo*.

2

I Have Called You Friends

I have called you friends.
John 15:15, NEB

The man who speaks will be dead and buried twenty-four hours later. He is preparing a small circle of his followers to be ready to live without him. He warns them that in their future life they will be partakers of the same conflict about to claim his life.

Remember the words I said to you:
A servant is not greater than his master.
If they persecuted me,
they will persecute you too;
if they kept my word,
they will keep yours as well.
But it will be on my account that they will do all this
because they do not know the one who sent me.
John 15:20-21, JB

So the reason for the hostility is "not knowing." This does not mean simple ignorance or lack of information. It means lack of acknowledgement. They do not recognize who sent Jesus.

If I had not come,
if I had not spoken to them,
they would have been blameless;
but as it is they have no excuse for their sin (*v. 22*).

Who is this "they"? These verses name no one. They don't name the Jews nor the Romans. The rejection Jesus describes is broader than that. He says it comes from "the world."

> If the world hates you,
>   remember that it hated me before you.
> If you belonged to the world,
>   the world would love you as its own;
> but because you do not belong to the world,
>   because my choice withdrew you from the world,
>   therefore the world hates you (*v. 19*).

What then is this "world" whose hatred is to be expected? It does not mean the globe. It does not mean God's good creation. It does not mean the rocks and streams and animal life. It does not mean "all the people."

The Greek word *cosmos* which is used here might best be translated "the system." It points to the way things fit together: to the networking, the organizing; to the way that God's refractory creation, God's rebellious creatures stick together for evil. Human solidarity is a good thing, but once solidarity has become nationalism, racism, collective selfishness, it is not. Human rationality is a good thing, but when it has been harnessed to destruction, it is not.

God made his creatures capable of organization through solidarity. When we use those capacities for evil, they still work. What is wrong with our world is not simply a matter of isolated individual ignorance or isolated evil will. It is not just that I am a sinner and you another, she a sinner, and they sinners, and it all adds up. The whole world is worse than the sum of its parts.

This is a first sobering truth about the task facing the peace movement. What killed Jesus was a *world*. The men who joined in executing Jesus were the mere instruments of larger forces. This is what the apostle Paul meant when he wrote:

> For it is not against human enemies
>   that we have to struggle,
> but against the Sovereignties

and the Powers who originate
the darkness in this world.
                              Ephesians 6:12, JB

It all hangs together. What President Eisenhower called "the military-industrial complex" is far more complex than that. It is not only the Pentagon and the owners of industry. It is not only also the banks, university researchers, labor organizers, political parties . . . it is all of us.

The "challenge of peace" is not, then, just a matter of fixing or fine-tuning a system of which the other parts are working well. We are not trying merely to correct one mistake in an otherwise adequate culture. We are dealing, rather, with an evil that is representative and prototypical. When you cut across a piece of wood you find a pattern of lines or circles that we call "the grain." The grain is not only at the end of the wood; it runs all the way through the log. You see it at the extremity where the cutting exposed it.

The arms race is like that. It is the cut that exposes the grain. The grain is national chauvinism, the assumption of moral superiority inherent in our kind of people and of the right to sacrifice the security of other people for the sake of our own. The grain that runs clear through the wood is trust in coercive power to bend others to our will. If we thought we could do that to our neighbors with crossbows or with slingshots instead of atomic weapons, that would be no better morally.

But organization and technology have so multiplied the stakes that anyone can see the grain. Anyone can see that the evil is systemic. That is why a particular tactic, such as a nuclear freeze, even if it is a good political first step, is not enough. It was not enough in the 19th century to stop importing slaves.

One mistake we need to avoid is placing the blame on some evil people. Most people within "the system" are not nasty. They do not beat their wives and children. A few of them are brutal; some are selfish or venal, profiteers or racketeers; but most of them are not. They may lack imagination or courage, just as I do.

Most of the people who ran Hitler's Reich were decent people. They were gentle with their children, and they kept their files in order. They followed the rules and worked hard. They were more hostages than villains.

The second mistake to avoid is thinking that the response to all of this evil ought to be hatred. The world hates God and Jesus and his disciples, but God does not hate the world. He loves the world; that is why he sent his Son to be its willing victim. In that connecton, with that goal of God's in mind, there is and can be and must be no ditch between Jesus and ourselves. Jesus loved his enemies (including us); we are to love our enemies. Jesus let that love cost him his life. We can risk the things we value, most of which are much less than life itself, for the sake of our enemies.

We noted at the beginning that the context of the cross is what gives this Scripture passage its meaning. Jesus is present in order to give himself willingly. He says that he is *sent.* His cause is not his own. The authority with which he acts is not his own. The Father stands behind his free choice to give himself. His will is the Father's will; his intention is the Father's. The God of the gospel, the God whom Jesus calls "Father," is a peacemaker, a reconciler.

This truth is not self-evident. In some strands of Christianity it is not affirmed—or it is even denied. In some strands of Christianity, the Father is strict and the Son is gentle. God the Father is a condemning judge, while the Son is an advocate pleading our cause, or even a substitute suffering in our stead under the anger of the Father. God the Father is a patriarch, whereas Jesus is a feminist.

It is important that we should correct that view. It is deeply rooted in our culture. It has to do with some people's views about death and war and enemies. The apostle Paul corrects that error when he writes:

> God was in Christ
> reconciling the world to himself,
> giving us the ministry of reconciliation.
>
> *2 Corinthians 5:19*

Jesus did have to die for us. He died to reveal the Father's compassion, not to appease the Father's love.

Jesus himself wards off that error when he says:

> Love your enemies
>   do good and lend
>   without hope of return.
> You will have a great reward,
>   and you will be sons of the Most High
>   [i.e., you will resemble God],
> for God is kind to the ungrateful and the wicked.
>
> *Luke 6:35*

That may be the first thing we need to make perfectly clear. Christian concern for peace is not an optional hobby of some softhearted people. It is not the product of a debatable reading of the accuracy of the technical assumptions built into the Pentagon's scenarios for preparedness.

Concern for peace, whether Jewish or Christian, is part of the purpose of God for all eternity. God is by nature a reconciler, a maker of shalom. For us to participate in the peacemaking purposes of that kind of God is not just morality. It is not just politics. It is worship, doxology, praise.

There are more ways than one for a person to do the will of another person. Jesus distinguishes here between two levels of relationship.

> One can have no greater love
>   than to lay down one's life for one's friends.
> You are my friends
>   if you do what I command you.
> I shall not call you servants anymore,
>   because a servant does not know
>   his master's business.
> I call you friends,
>   because I have made known to you
>   everything I have learned from my Father.
>
> *John 15:13ff.*

The disciples, then, did not just obey orders. The word here translated *servant* means more literally *slave*. Sometimes that term is used to describe Christian obedience to God as master. But here the difference is that a slave is one who does not know the master's purpose. He knows what his own orders are, and obeys them, but does not know the complete plan. He does not know why obedience makes sense. So when Jesus says, "I have given you the title of *friends*," he means that we are in on what it is all about. We know the battle plan behind our service.

The apostle Paul was saying something similar in his letter to the Ephesians, when he wrote about the divine mystery hidden through the ages but now revealed through the apostles and prophets. We have the privilege of being in on God's purposes. We are not pawns sovereignly moved about on a cosmic chessboard. We are the players.

Now we can grasp more fully the weight of the statements with which we began. "The world will treat you as it is treating me." Jesus says. The peacemaking work of the believer, in conflict, in suffering, is a continuation of the work of Christ. The apostle Paul said of himself, "I fill out what was lacking in the sufferings of Christ" (Colossians 1:25).

The letter of John says,

> Do not be like Cain
>   who cut his brother's throat. . . .
> He has taught us love
>   in that he gave up his life for us.
> We, too, ought to give up our lives for our brothers.
> *1 John 3:12-16*

Our teachers have often drawn the line separating salvation from obedience, dividing what Jesus did for us from what we are to do for him. That line is real. It is appropriate for some valid religious purposes. If the question were whether we can save ourselves, or whether God owes us some reward for our works, that line would matter. But that is not our question. Our question is how we can honor God the peacemaker. How can we intelligibly participate in God's purposes, as *friends* who are in on his battle plan? How can we knowingly and responsibly participate in his peacemaking project for the planet?

Originally presented on March 26, 1983, at Franciscan Life Center, Sylvania, Ohio.

3

The Wisdom and The Power

The language of the cross may be illogical
    to those who are not on the way to salvation,
but those of us who are on the way
    see it as God's power to save.
As scripture says:
I shall destroy the wisdom of the wise
    and bring to nothing
    all the learning of the learned.
Where are the philosophers now?. . .
Where are any of our thinkers today?
Do you see now how God has shown up
    the foolishness of human wisdom?
If it was God's wisdom that human wisdom should not know God,
it was because God wanted to save those who have faith
through the foolishness of the message that we preach.
And so, while the Jews demand miracles
    and the Greeks look for wisdom,
here are we preaching a crucified Christ;
to the Jews an obstacle that they cannot get over,
to the pagans madness,
but to those who have been called,
    whether they are Jews or Greeks,
a Christ who is the power and the wisdom of God.
For God's foolishness is wiser than human wisdom,
and God's weakness is stronger than human strength.

1 Corinthians 1:18-25, JB

The apostle Paul is no anthropologist. When he speaks here of *Jew* and of *Greek* he is not saying that a specific race—even less a specific religion—makes its members all the same. He is speaking about mental types represented then—more or less—by different ethnic communities, and present in amy age. We are all more or less *Greek* and more or less *Jewish* in this sense.

When Paul says, "The Jews demand a sign," he is speaking not so much of a religion or of a race as of a culture. By *Jew* he does not mean somebody like Woody Allen; he means people who want to see proofs of God's power. The *sign* is an evidence of power. The people in the Gospels were asking Jesus for a sign to accredit his ministry. They wanted the kind of performance from him that would save them from the risk of trusting him by assuring them that God was his side.

There have been cultures in which power was less important than something else: pleasure or wisdom, wealth or sex. But in the heritage of Abraham, Moses, David, and Elijah, Jews and Christians have learned to expect God to act powerfully in the interest of justice. Other religions may see the world as static and history as cyclical; the children of Abraham see it as drawn ahead by promises and driven by memories of past deliverances. The prophets proclaim God at work. Zealots help God with his victory. Christian emperors and crusaders triumph in his name. The empire spreads his glory around the world.

For good and for ill we are their heirs. We ask of a command, "Will it work?" and of a moral principle, "What will it produce?" If we are told to renounce violence, we ask, "But then what should we do if someone threatens our friends or our values?" Nationally we ask, "What would you do if the Russians came?" or "How would we keep the peace if no one would defend the country?"

The Hebrews differ from the Hindus, for whom divine power and light are diffused through multiple complex and contradictory forms. They differ from the Buddhists, for whom the power of events in historical experience needs to be downplayed or even denied. And they differ from tribal cultures where no change is expected and the gods are the guardians of stability. The JHWH of the Hebrews is a mover and shaker. At Sinai he was known in a storm cloud. He saved his people from Pharaoh by mobilizing the sea. The God of Joshua, of the judges, of Saul and David helped his people—against their enemies—by mighty saving acts.

Mary was told that her child should be named Joshua (Jesus), because he would liberate his people. It was no surprise that some thought of such liberation after the model of Moses and Joshua, or after the more recent model of the Maccabean revolt, which had for a while set up Jewish priests as kings of an independent Israel.

Some people in Jesus' time wanted him to take that path. For them the weakness of the cross was a barrier to faith. There were still such people in Paul's time. When Paul was taken prisoner in Jerusalem, we read that the Roman tribune mistook him at first for the leader of a group of four thousand nationalist rebels. A decade later Jerusalem was in fact "liberated" by one Menahem, who held it against the Romans for a few months, and provoked the city's destruction.

So when Paul says, "The Jews want a sign," that is the precedent for the visions of national renewal by means of military upheaval which today are destroying Central America and the Middle East, Eritrea and Chad. We will believe God is with us when we win.

But Jesus did not win. Any death is defeat of a kind, but crucifixion was worse than that. The Romans did not crucify petty thieves or murderers. It was the penalty for rebels. Jesus' death was the dramative defeat of a movement leader.

That fact is still a stumbling block. How can we believe in God if he is not our helper? How can Jesus be Lord if he is defeated?

One true answer to that kind of question is to say that Christian love is not so ineffective as all that. There are things that love alone can get done. There are kinds of nonviolent process which are quite effective in achieving valuable goals.

A social science called *conflict resolution* demonstrates that there are better and worse ways, which can be analyzed and learned, to defend valid interests. It can be shown as a fact of social science that massing destructive threat against destructive threat postpones the solution of problems, even if the war never happens, to say nothing of destroying most of what both parties wanted to save, if it does come.

Gandhi and King demonstrated the power of truth made effective through active noncooperation with evil. It is costly, though hardly more costly than war. To recognize the sacredness of the adversary's life and dignity, to refuse to meet him on his own terms, is at once a moral victory and the beginning of a tactical advantage—but you will only do it if you believe.

But the best answer to those questions, according to our text, would be to say that the question is wrong. It is wrong to be scandalized by the cross as weakness, because it is wrong to demand strength. It is wrong to assume that the measure of right decision or the validation of correct behavior is its power to make events come out right. To claim that it is our right, or that it is even our duty, or that it is within our capability to take charge of events to assure the results we consider desirable, is by no means so simply true as we always assume.

Yet only if one does assume such a right, such a duty, and such a capability, does the notion that the cross is weakness have to follow. This assumption explains that dissatisfaction with the cross as powerless which lies at the heart of the "scandalized" reaction of those who ask for "a sign."

The cross of Jesus, the crucifixion as it happened in history, was not the result of any decision to be weak or of any sacrifice of the will. It was the product of the firmness with which Jesus held to the path to which he had been called. Crucifixion was the normal result of who he was and how he acted, in the face of the powers of this world whose rule over mankind he challenged. One who acts and speaks as he did will be treated as he was treated. It takes strength and hope to act that way, not weakness.

The cross of Christ later comes to have other meanings. It may be spoken about as penalty, as sacrifice, or as victory. But all such additional depths of meaning derive from and are dependent upon the social and historical one: a righteous man was put to death because of the way he refused to let stand the unrighteousness of the powers in control of the people he came to liberate. It is also the way he calls his followers to take. That is what causes us to stumble: not that the cross is weak but that it asks of us too much strength.

When Paul says that "the Greeks ask for wisdom," again he is describing not a race or a nationality but a culture. By Greek he does not mean someone like Zorba. Nor does he mean all his readers in Corinth, the Greek city. He means to identify a mode of moral reasoning. Greek was the language of culture and of philosophy, even in Rome and in Egypt.

When he says "the Greeks ask for wisdom," he is putting his finger on a way of reasoning which we have all learned.

All of our culture since then is indebted to the fathers of Greek philosophy, for the ability to ask regularly and rigorously, "But is that always true? Is it true for everyone?" We have learned to ask that truth be validated by its being general and not just particular, by its being true for everyone, not dependent upon perspective or bias. The philosopher Kant told us to ask of a moral statement whether it could be true for everyone. Democracy teaches us to consider as right what most people will vote for. Scholarship teaches us to respect the consensus of authorities. Truth is suspect if it cannot be commended to everyone.

When we apply that perspective to the Christian's obligation to love the enemy, questions follow: "Can you ask that of everyone? Can you convince people that it will work? Does it not strike people as counter to common sense? Is it not most credible if you agree to label it as a rare peculiarity of a minority denomination, not to be asked or expected of others? Is it not irrelevant as guidance for the whole society?"

Paul does not agree with the "Greeks" that the word of the cross is foolish, but he understands how they see it that way. He points out further that such wisdom does not in general facilitate people's becoming believers:

Take yourselves, for instance:
How many of you were wise, influential, noble,
when you were called? (1:26)

God's message runs across the grain of our sense-making reflexes becaue they are tilted in our favor. What we call "reasonable" is against sacrifice and for self-preservation, against trusting and for demanding explanations, against risk, against the outsider and the enemy.

Two hundred and thirty Catholic bishops issue a pastoral letter on "The Challenge of Peace," and we say, "But they aren't
expert. Would there be no exceptions? What theory of human nature and of government is presupposed by such an appeal?"

The human spirit is a sense-making organ, and that certainly
is a good thing. We learn to test thoughts for their consistency.
But, unfortunately, that skill can run away with us if we try to
handle situations that are different in the same manner. Or we
can assume that something we don't know everything about must
be false.

We need not concede that a peace commitment is sectarian,
irrelevant, or illogical. It is, in fact, possible to argue for love of
neighbor on the grounds of the general wisdom of an ancient
philosophical consensus, and the lessons of the history of the race,
and what will make sense to most rational beings thinking carefully. But at the outset we cannot and should not attempt to vali-
date the love of enemy by such criteria, as if our using such arguments were to be taken as granting that they have a final authority.

The gospel of Christ is not obscurantist. It does not ask for
blind faith, but it does ask for confession. It does not spare us the
decision to recognize Christ as Lord. That decision is not made for
us by the facts of the case, or by our parents, or by some irresisti-
ble logical proof. We sometimes try to avoid the risk of faith for
our children by telling them that there is no other choice—that
faith is unavoidable. That used to be convincing in a society
dominated by the churches.

Jesus, on the other hand, warned his listeners that they

should not follow him unless they were ready to suffer, as he was going to suffer.

The disciples of Jesus are a minority, not because particular doctrines that they hold on the ground of particular revelatory experiences are not convincing to others. "The Greeks" could have respected that kind of special information. The disciples of Jesus are an unpopular minority because they love their enemies as Jesus did, and because their commitment to this path does not depend on its prior acceptability to others. It is not that they choose to be foolish but that they are committed to another standard of wisdom.

Sometime in August of 1525, in the midst of a frustrating debate about infant baptism in the office of the Swiss reformer Oecolampadius, one of the Anabaptist participants said: "What is needed is divine wisdom in order to see honor in the cross and life in death; we must deny ourselves and become fools."

He was quoting our text, repeating a well-worn argument, familiar in the medieval pursuit of mystical insight and in the Protestant argument against the scholastic church. What he was calling for, and what Paul is calling for, is not mysticism as over against reason, nor blind faith as over against scholarship. What they called for is the understanding that the cross of Christ is in fact a new definition of truth, both as power and as wisdom.

One way all of us, both Jews and Greeks, seek to avoid this call is to redefine "following Jesus" so that it focuses on some point other than the cross. Like the famous Pastor Henry Maxwell in the best-selling Christian novel *In His Steps*, we transform "doing what Jesus would do" into doing with integrity and courage whatever we actually think is right in a particular situation. Or with the heritage of St. Francis we can simplify our lifestyle, go barefoot and beg. Yet the early Christians did not make Jesus an example in his celibacy, or in his not having a gainful occupation or a domicile—only in his cross.

The other way of escape is to give great importance to the cross, but to give it some other meaning. In Christian pastoral care we speak of a person having a cross to bear and mean by that some conflict in interpersonal relations, or some intractable sickness or handicap. An accident or an illness may be called a "cross."

In yet another school of pastoral care the cross symbolizes the experience of death to self: the discipline which in mystical or devotional exercises one can undergo as a part of becoming a Jesuit or a Quaker or a Wesleyan.

Or it is possible to move the cross from the realm of pastoral care to that of theology. In the theology of the sacraments, this has led to the debate about the miracle of transubstantiation. In the realm of sin and grace it refers to the miracle of atonement. In the realm of history one can puzzle over the historical details of the Gospel accounts. In interdisciplinary dialogue one can reinterpret the event through Freudian, or Nietzschian, or Marxist grids.

Some of these alternative understandings of what the cross is about are quite right in their place; others are more questionable. Yet none of them is appropriate if understood as a replacement, rather than a reinforcement, of the call to share with Jesus the path of incarnate love—God in mankind (incarnation) meeting mankind against God (rebellion) at God's expense (atonement).

The alternative vision of the entire matter which for Paul is fundamental is not merely to see that sometimes suffering love is powerful enough to effect social change. (Some of our neighbors are more ready to recognize this truth after the work of Gandhi and King.) Rather, in his very failure and death we confess that God was moving omnipotently to reverse the stream of history which since Cain had been under the sign of hostility.

If the cross is wisdom, we can learn to read history differently, namely from below. We can read ethics differently. We can see that the measure of the true reasonableness of a deed is not whether everyone agrees or whether if enough others did it, we would win. Rather, the measure is whether that deed (or the quality of will and purpose it displays) is congruent with the divine character manifested in the cross, and also everywhere else in healthy life: in patient mothering, in painful truth-telling, in honest brokering, and in mutually respectful problem-solving.

If the cross is power we can learn to participate in history differently—in hope. Sometimes, like the early Christians, or like the Jews in Babylon to whom Jeremiah wrote, or like the Anabaptist heroes of the sixteenth century in the *Martyrs Mirror*, we shall need simply to "take it on faith" that our weakness fits into the Lamb's victory. But such faith will not be a grim or resentful perseverance. It will be service in hope, marked by the trust in God's already certain triumph that marks the hymns of the fifth chapter of Revelation.

Sometimes, like the Friends who helped open seventeenth-century England to the rights of dissent and of prisoners, and eighteenth-century America to the rights of the Indians, we will see our suffering giving us a share in the already incipient construction of a less brutal world. We may see our weakness as that of a strategic minority which, by virtue of its creativity, or of its taking up a task no one else had seen, or of its location at the hinge between the power blocs, can self-consciously maneuver its participation in the welfare of its wider society.

The shape of the challenge is misunderstood whenever Christians believe (as many have) that they are called by the law of love to leave the field to the adversary, and to grant that human wisdom and power may continue autonomous in their own realms, since God's wisdom and power are something else. That is not what the text says. It says that human understandings of power fail to recognize the real power of God in and for real historical experience, in and through the cross. People are proven wrong who believe that by escalating their capacity to destroy those one has ceased to dialogue with as fellow humans they will in fact make the course of events come out the way they want it to in their own territory on their own terms: "Where are kings and empires now of old that went and came?"

Only in recent decades have social scientists begun to inventory the ways in which a soft answer turns away wrath, but it has always been true. It is only in our epoch of nationwide media and movements that charismatic leaders like Gandhi and King can develop a technology of nonviolent social struggle. But it was true before their time that the way to make peace is not to make war.

The cross was, after all, not an event outside the realm of politics. The largest, best-organized, and relatively most just empire in world history was executing a nonviolent teacher on the grounds that he represented a threat of national liberation. We would not be reading the story today if it had not turned out that:

> Though the cause of evil prosper,
>   yet 'tis truth alone is strong;
> Though her portion be the scaffold
>   and upon the throne be Wrong,
> Yet that scaffold sways the future,
>   and, behind the dim unknown,
>   standeth God within the shadow,
>   keeping watch above his own.

> *James Russell Lowell,*
> adapted for use as a hymn

This was probably the text most often cited by Martin Luther King, Jr., in the face of the persistent power of evil.

The cross is what makes sense of life, even if to our neighbors—and to our doubting selves—it looks crazy. The cross is what makes history move, even if we've been told the opposite in our national mythology, according to which world leadership is measured in megatonnage, and in our media morality dramas, where every plot problem is resolved by a gun, and in our local economic dramas, where every employment problem is resolved by a federal weapons contract.

> It was to shame the wise that God chose what is
>   foolish by human reckoning;
> and to shame the strong that he chose
>   what is weak by human reckoning. . . .
> The human race has nothing to boast about. . . .
>   If anyone wants to boast, let him boast about the Lord.

> *1 Corinthians 1:27-31, JB*

Spoken first at Montevideo, Uruguay, April 1971. Adapted most recently at the First Presbyterian Church of Cedar Rapids, Iowa.

4

What Are You Doing More Than They?

If you love those who love you,
  Do not the tax gatherers do the same?
And if you greet your brothers,
  What more are you doing?
    Do not the ethnics do the same?

Matthew 5:46-48

Jesus is not talking about the difference between pacifists and other Christians, or between peace-church evangelism and some other kind of evangelism. Jesus is talking about the difference between people who listen to him and those who do not.

Those who do not, whom he calls "they," have three names:
—tax gatherers
—sinners (the term used in Luke's Gospel)
—ethnics
This word *ethnic* is used only four times in the New Testament. It does not mean a Gentile, who is identified as such by the fact that he is not a Jew. A Gentile may be a disciple of Jesus. The term (also translatable as *pagan* or *heathen*) refers rather, to one whose character is marked by his being outside the people of God, or by his being loyal to some other community.

Now if Jesus is talking about what it is that makes a difference when some people are disciples, he is on the subject of evangelism. He says that there is about the life of the disciple a difference, a quality of *moreness*.

In Matthew 5:46 identifies this quesion of moreness by asking, "What reward have you?" In the parallel according to Luke, the question is, "What thanks would be due to you?" In verse 47 he simply asks, "What more are you doing?" He does not ask, "What are you doing more than others?" as the King James version has it, nor "more than they," as our title has it. He is rather asking, "What is the *greater thing* you are doing?"

So this is our topic: "How does the moreness of the gospel way of life contribute to our understanding of the meaning of evangelism?"

Newness

This word of Jesus is the climax of a series of six paragraphs, each of which began, "You have heard . . . but *I* say to you. . . ."

That series in turn is the unfolding of the beginning statement, "I have come to fulfill the law." That statement in its turn is based on the Beatitudes. The whole chapter, this entire sequence of thoughts linked into one another, is based upon or stands on the shoulders of the narrative account of Matthew 4 which tells us about Jesus' baptism, about the voice from heaven giving him his distinct call, about his testing in the desert, and then about his beginning to proclaim the kingdom of God and to heal people. It would be worth looking at every step along this passage to ask what each means for evangelism. Every one of those steps in the account of Matthew—the baptism, the voice, the testing, the first preaching—would tell us something we need to know about how to proclaim the gospel or what the gospel is. Here, however, we must limit ourselves to two observations.

First, Jesus is proclaiming *a kingdom that is at hand.* He is not merely instructing people in a body of ideas and doctrines (although ideas and doctrines will be implied and cannot be avoided). He is not inviting people primarily to a personal experience (although you cannot respond to his message without its being personal and an experience).

What he is announcing is a whole new order of things. To describe it, he uses political language; his preferred term is "kingdom." It is a new set of *relationships*. It involves healing and other mighty works. It is a *movement* which includes drawing people away from their regular occupations to come with him. Some will even permanently leave their prior occupations to be part of his serving community.

The second observation we make about the text is more difficult because it calls us to be careful about words. What do we mean by *beatitude*? You are familiar with the text. Eight times Jesus says, "Blessed are ye if . . . because. . . ."

We tend to take this list of "blessings" as a list of virtues that good people have, or of deeds that good people do. In other words it is a kind of moral demand: "Do this, and if you do you will get such and such reward." That's the way most of us understand the text. But this cannot be its full and proper meaning. Some of these attitudes that Jesus says you will be blessed in are not deeds you can "up and do." You cannot decide, "Now I am going to mourn." You cannot decide, "Now I am going to hunger and thirst for righteousness." These are not actions for which rewards are announced. These are rather postures or attitudes in which people already find themselves when the kingdom comes.

A second reason for not considering the Beatitudes as a list of moral demands is that then their meaning as gospel would be lost. There would be no link to the proclaiming of the kingdom as good news. Still a further consideration is the literal meaning of the word *makarios*, "blessed." It does not mean "you shall be rewarded" or "you shall find some recompense." It means, rather, "Happy are you!" or "Good for you!"

In other words, Jesus is saying,

"There are already people in the world who are sorrowful. Good for them! Because the kingdom is now here and they shall be comforted!

"There are already people whose hearts are pure. Good for

them! Because the kingdom is coming and they shall see God!

"There are those who claim nothing, the meek. Good for them! Because the kingdom is around the corner and the whole earth will be theirs!"

(This same observation is even more clear when compared to the text of Luke. There the blessings are paired with an equal number of woes: "Woe to you who laugh now, for you shall weep. Woe to you who are full now for you shall be hungry." Here it is even more clear that the meaning cannot be one of teaching ethics. It is rather proclamation of the meaning of the coming of the rule of God.)

This clarification about the meaning of *beatitude* leads us to a first conclusion about the moreness of the gospel. It is a beatitude, a blessedness, a privilege, a good deal, a gift, a result of the kingdom's coming.

Evangelism means to say and to believe that it is *good news.* But is it not true that most of us have thought otherwise? Among many peace church Christians a different set of assumptions is at work. We tend to assume that the central evangelistic message is good news and is free with no questions asked. First get forgiveness and love and peace of soul. Then you begin to follow Jesus. Then comes the fine print, the hard part, the next step.

You may have learned to talk about this "next step" as a process of nurture or sanctification that you have to work at. Or you may have been taught that it will come automatically, that it is a by-product of the faith. In any case, we have been taught that this further step or further process, the demands of the gospel, will be more clear if the two steps are held apart. The moreness of the gospel life is the second step, the hard one, the bad news that comes after the good news.

This is not what Jesus says. He says it is all good news. He says it is by grace through faith that peacemakers are the children of God, and that is a joyful message because it is part of the kingdom coming. That those who hunger and thirst for righteousness shall be filled is *good news,* because the kingdom is at hand.

The same point is evident from another side as well. We live in a society that largely claims to be Christian, with chaplains in the armed forces and in the houses of Congress, with school prayer amendments in the Congress, with godly slogans on our money and postage stamps. And yet no *one* church is official. The result of this is the assumption that there are two levels to being Christian. One is the basics, the common denominator, the agreed minimum requirement. This is what it takes to be Christian, or to be a Christian; and then there are the additional options, the folkloric furbelows:

—The Anglicans add bishops.

—The Baptists add more water.

—The Wesleyans add holiness.

—The evangelicals add correct doctrine.

—The Pentecostals add spirit.

—The peace churches add their thing.

All of these options, added to the basic minimum of the Protestant cultural heritage, are called "distinctives." It is considered good to have them, but they are not fundamental. The automobile dealer would call them pizzazz. The sociologist will call them folklore. They add character and individuality and taste, but they don't really matter.

Once you understand things this way, which of the levels is the gospel? Is it the minimum requirement? Or is it the more, the second mile?

Some of us have obviously tended to assume the former. The gospel is the minimum to which more will be added. The gospel is the common American Protestant message, which is more acceptable and more essential and more powerful if we leave off the options when presenting it.

But Jesus seems to be saying it the other way around. For him the distinctives identify the gospel. Evangelism, good news, is proclaiming precisely the plus, the otherness, the moreness, the noncomformity of the church as a visible city on a hill. It is the savor of the salt. It is the greater righteousness that fulfills the law, which people see and glorify our heavenly Father.

The plus quality of the life according to the gospel is more

than a *result* of the gospel. It is more than a *verification* or confir-
mation of the gospel. It is also the *communication* of the gospel. It
is evangelism. It is the distinctives, in fact, which identify the
message.

Jesus is not saying, "Be good, be different, be nonconformed,
and people will see how good you are. They will want to have
what you have." No, their attention, according to the passage, is
drawn not to us but to the Father. Yet attention is drawn to the
Father, not by a new set of words, but by a new kind of life.

We must be careful. The differentness that attracts people is
not just any old differentness, not just a "Hey, look!" symbolic
call for attention. The distinctiveness Jesus is talking about is not
like a Salvation Army uniform or a clergyman's collar, or plain
garb, which tells you "here is somebody set apart," but does not
tell you why or how they differ. The differentness with Jesus, the
differentness which says something is itself the message.

If I am the child of a Father who loves both good and evil
children, if I am witness for a God who loves his enemies, then
when I love my enemy I am *proclaiming* that love. I am not just
obeying it; I am communicating it. And I cannot communicate it
any other way.

The enemy whom I love, the person coercing me with whom
I go a second mile, experiences through me the call to accept
grace, because my action makes God's forgiveness real. No other
way could do that.

If I lovingly go the second mile, or turn the other cheek to
someone who struck me, I am speaking God's forgiving love in
the form of the situation by standing before him defenseless.

So it would be with the rest of the Sermon on the Mount. If,
as Jesus calls us to do, we forsake our goods to follow him, we are
proclaiming our trust in a Father who knows our needs. If, as he
tells us to do, we tell the truth without varnish, without oaths and
asseverations, we proclaim the sanctity of the name of God and of
truthfulness. If, as he tells us to, we forsake self-defense, we
preach that Christ, and not the ruler with the biggest army, is the
Lord of history.

Thus far I have been quoting Jesus. I have been trying to take the New Testament message straight. But the plus quality of the gospel acquires additional meanings as time passes. We have yet to watch how that meaning changes from biblical times until now.

Especially, new meanings arise with the development of official Christianity (religion identified with the nation, with the state, with the world).

After the development of official religion, when we hear Jesus warning against "greeting only our brothers the way the ethnics do," his call takes on a new dimension. If Christianity is an *official* religion, it means that we can follow Jesus only by rejecting that kind of Christianity. We can call people to the Jesus Christ of the gospel only by calling them away from the "Christ" they already know—away from the official, conformist, power-related religion of the West. This is the meaning of reformation. Henceforth—since Constantine and Charlemagne—the cutting edge of gospel proclamation must include the rejection of the abuse of Christianity by those who identify it with the selfishness or the self-fulfillment of a nation or a race, a culture or a class.

In the context of the officially established religion that prevailed when the peace church movements were born, or in the context of an unofficially established religion which prevails today, it is not enough to call people to confess Jesus Christ as Lord. He himself threw back the question; "Why do you call me Lord and not do what I say?"

Even to those who point to good deeds done in his name he will say, "I never knew you."

The gospel for tomorrow must be spoken as nonconformity, as judgment upon conformed religion, as judgment upon conformist Jesus talk, even as judgment on conformist evangelism and on patriotic piety or it will not be good news. it must smash the idols of self-satisfying, self-saving religion or it will not be able to save.

Jesus says, "If you greet your friends, what *more* are you doing? Do not the nationalists do as much?" What does that mean when nationalism has been Christianized or Christianity nationalized? What does it mean *for evangelism?*

I suggest that it must mean far more than simply hoping that if some individuals hear our message and are converted, some of them will love their enemies. The meaning of the moreness of the gospel must begin with the message. This must not await the exceptional personal pilgrimage of the individual who hears and responds. The message itself must undercut establishment religion.

The message itself must denounce and undercut nationalism and ethnocentrism in a host of different ways:

—by repeating that Jesus was a Jew and a Galilean
—by affirming the dignity of the outsider and the outcast
—by rejecting in the name of the Spirit of Pentecost every identification of the gospel with a single culture or language
—by including the sins of the comfortable among those from which God saves people instead of limiting our illustrations of the power of the gospel to the sins of the young and the weak
—by going out to look for what God is doing outside our own world and celebrating it.

The gospel does not only *imply* an ethic of peacemaking or being set at peace, nor does it merely *lead to* a nonviolent lifestyle. It *proclaims* a reconciled view of the world. Phillips' version of Ephesians translates Paul this way:

For he reconciled both [Jew and Greek, insider and outsider] to God by the sacrifice of one body on the cross and by this act made utterly irrelevant the antagonism between them. Then he came and told both you who were far from God [the outsider, the Gentile] and us who were near [the insiders, the Jews] that the war was over.

Ephesians 2:14-17

That is the gospel—not that *war is sin.* That also is true, but alone it would not be the gospel. The gospel is that *the war is over.* Not merely that you *ought* to love your enemy. Not merely that if you have had a "born-again experience," some of your hate feelings will go away and you maybe *can* love. Not merely that if you deal with your enemies lovingly enough, some of them will become friendly. All of that is true, but it is not the gospel. The gospel is that everyone being loved by God must be my beloved too, even if they consider me their enemy, even if their interests clash with mine.

"If anyone is in Christ [the *New English Bible* translates it correctly] "there is a whole new world" (2 Corinthians 5:17). Evangelism is not a call to have a new feeling or a new idea or even a new self-image. It is the call to discover and to accept a whole new world. That is the meaning of the "righteousness greater than that of the scribes and Pharisees." That is for today what it means to "do more than they." It is not a matter merely a higher moral demand. Churches are good at moral demands. This is a matter not of a greater demand, but of a greater supply, a bigger gospel, a broader grasp of what grace wants to do and already has done by calling perspms to return to be God's children.

For some of us, everything that matters for evangelism and renewal of the church depends on the key question of the authority of the Bible. And that is probably right.

For others of us, everything depends on rediscovering the real, lively presence of the Holy Spirit. And that is probably right.

For still others it depends on clarifying our view of ministry, or on learning sensitivity in group process, or on a new kind of Christian education, and perhaps those things are right too. All of these are offered to us, or are asked of us, by the New Testament. If any one of them is really missing, the gospel becomes spurious. And yet there must be "more."

> People of any nation, any culture,
> greet their brothers and sisters;
> and lend money for good risks;
> and feed their families;
> and recruit converts for their movements.

But your love must be gospel:
    your helping must be grace.
    Your response to hostility must be reconciliation;
    your movement must be outward;
    your gospel invitation must be to newness of life . . . .

Why?
    Because that's the way it is. That's the good news.
    Because that is the way God is.

Spoken at Probe 1976, Minneapolis. Printed in *Mennonite Life* 1977.

5

The Voice of Your Brother's Blood

Now Abel became a shepherd and kept flocks,
  while Cain tilled the soil.
Time passed and Cain brought some of the produce of the soil as
  an offering for Yahweh,
while Abel for his part brought the first-born of his flock and some
  of their fat as well.
Yahweh looked with favor on Abel and his offering.
But he did not look with favor on Cain and his offering,
  and Cain was very angry and downcast.
Yahweh asked Cain, "Why are you angry and downcast?
  If you are well disposed, ought you not to lift up your head?
  But if you are ill disposed, is not sin at the door like a crouching
    beast hungering for you, which you must master?"
Cain said to his brother Abel, "Let us go out,"
And while they were in the open country, Cain set on his brother
  Abel and killed him.

Yahweh asked Cain, "Where is your brother Abel?"
"I do not know" he replied.
"Am I my brother's guardian?"
"What have you done?" Yahweh asked.
"Listen to the sound of your brother's blood, crying out to me
  from the ground. Now be accursed and driven from the ground
  that has opened its mouth to receive your brother's blood at
  your hands. When you till the ground it shall no longer yield

you any of its produce. You shall be a fugitive and wanderer
over the earth."
Then Cain said to Yahweh, "My punishment is greater than I can
bear.
See! Today you drive me from this ground.
I must hide from you, and be a fugitive and a wanderer over the
earth.
Why, whoever comes across me will kill me!"
"Very well, then," Yahweh replied, "if anyone kills Cain, seven-
fold vengeance shall be taken for him."
So Yahweh put a mark on Cain,
    to prevent whoever might come across him
    from striking him down.
Cain left the presence of Yahweh and settled in the land of Nod,
east of Eden.

Genesis 4:2-16, JB

Numerous questions surround this story, which we might
like to figure out but cannot. Where did both Cain and Abel get
the idea of sacrificing to God? Why was the sacrifice of Cain not
accepted? How did he know it was not accepted? The reason it
was not accepted may not have been his wrong attitude, because
we are not told that Cain was angry. We are told that he brought
a sacrifice.

There are other, deeper things we might like to figure out,
and perhaps could, but not for the purposes of this chapter.
Herdsmen and farmers have been in conflict throughout the history of civilization. There has also always been conflict between
country and city. Cain leaves farming and founds a city. His descendants were metalworkers and musicians. Obviously, the
writer of Genesis saw this all as somehow connected. Yet for our
purposes, we limit ourselves to the theme of life and death in the
text.

The history of society began with the shedding of innocent
blood. The human in history is by nature victim and murderer. As
soon as we know ourselves socially, as soon as we know that we are
social animals, we know that we are guilty socially. We know that
the harmony between humans and their natural environment has

been disturbed. It is from the soil that the voice of blood cries out. The security of personal life is disrupted. Cain complains that all who see him will seek to kill him. Urbanization—the creation of cities—with the representative skills of metalworking and music—is seen as the culmination not of human solidarity or of reconciliation but of estrangement. The city is not the product of a town's growing large; it is founded by a fugitive. From this we could unfold a whole book about the theology of culture.

When God responds to Cain's attack against the peace of his creation, he does not do it with an announcement or a decree. Just a question: "Where is your brother?" In the preceding chapter Adam was ashamed when God asked him about himself: "Adam, where are *you?*" Here, Cain thought that he had gotten away with killing his brother, out there in the country where no one knew. Now it is the brother God asks about. Adam had answered by passing on the blame to the woman. Cain is more flippant: "Am I the shepherd of the shepherd?" In each case the divine question was enough to make the guilty man answer guiltily.

The question is sufficient to unveil the facts. God does not impart any new information. He comes to look for Cain and the facts rise up to meet him.

> "What have you done?" Yahweh asks. "Listen to the sound of your brother's blood, crying out to me from the ground. Now be accursed! Be driven from the ground that has opened its mouth to receive your brother's blood at your hands."

Cain's guilt is not something that God proclaims or evaluates.

There might be something for us to learn from this. Some of us are deeply concerned about "secularization," as we see a society developing with little religious knowledge or sentiment. We ask: How can people be expected to hear a religious message if they have no religious background? How can people be expected to be concerned about the evils of war if they don't have a peace church background? How can people be expected to know that they are sinners if nobody has told them the rules they have broken?

Part of the answer might be here. Ask the person where his brother or sister is, and the answer will betray guilt. Come into the human situation, looking for the brother and the sister, and the voice of their blood will cry out from the ground when you ask the question.

We don't need a full theory of how to resolve all the problems of race relations. Just *look* at the urban ghetto. Just hear God's question, "Where is your brother?" and you will hear yourself answering with Cain's question, "Is that my business?" It was not necessary in the 1960s to have full journalistic information about Vietnam, or about how the United States had become involved in the conflict. It was sufficient to ask about our brothers and sisters, and we knew we could not hide what we had done.

When Cain turns against his brother man, he has destroyed the possibility of wholesome society:

> "You shall be a fugitive and a wanderer over the earth." Cain says to Yahweh: "My punishment is greater than I can bear. See! Today you drive me from this ground. I must hide from you, and be a fugitive and a wanderer over the earth. Whoever comes across me will kill me."

The possibility of wholesome society is replaced by the fate of a society based upon vengeance. Still, that is better than nothing, or than chaos. God gives Cain a sign, we are told, which enables life to go on, under the protection of the menace that anyone who would kill him would in turn be avenged.

Yet that vengeance easily runs away with itself. That is the immediate next step in the narrative. Cain's descendant Lamech rejoices that whereas the vengeance promised to protect Cain had been sevenfold, Lamech avenges himself seventy-sevenfold. A threat that was supposed to be protection (and in this text is not reported ever to have been carried out) has now become with Lamech a matter of pride.

Isn't that the way it is today? In our culture everyone

reserves the right of self-defense. Both in practice and in the basic moral code of our culture, it is possible to contemplate getting rid of another person if that person threatens me. Not many of us really do it. But neither are there many who would never do it or who would never contemplate it.

Sometimes this retaliation or deterrence is carried out with the supposed justification that it is based on a threat or a previous offense (the bad guy has to shoot first), sometimes not. Cain thought he had a reason: Abel's competition for the favor of God. As a result of the way we have all been taught to reserve the right of self-defense, no one can really trust anyone fully. We are protected not by mutual trust but by mutual fear. We are kept from doing still worse by the knowledge that vengeance is likely to be worse than the offense.

That is still a kind of protection. Most people feel safe. And, in general, people really are safer where there is any kind of government, even a tyrannical, vengeful one, than where there is not.

Yet the justified violence of government is always open to abuse. Just as the protection of Cain escalated into the brutality of Lamech, so today the claims our government makes to be our protector tend to escalate into the serious menace of uncontrollable wholesale destruction. One obvious example of this phenomenon is the one we lived through in the 1960s: the best possible argument for the destruction of Vietnam was the claim to be defending, without their invitation, the right of self-determination for the people of that country.

It was the earth that received the blood of Abel, and it was the earth that was cursed for Cain. Our violence toward one another also breaks our unity with nature. Just as in Genesis the sin against God, the abuse of the tree of life, resulted in expulsion from the garden, so today the fruitfulness of the land is jeopardized by hostility between us. We notice occasionally how our society is dependent on nature, and how the shape of the soils or the snows or the floods influences our well-being, but we seldom analyze deeply enough to know how much our land is being abused in the name of our civilization. As the word indicates, *cult*ivation, what Cain was the first to do, is the first form of *cult*ure. To develop a fruitful field demands years of cooperation between the farmer and his land, his learning how to nurture it, how to adjust the crops to the soils and the calendar. Cain cannot be a farmer if he cannot be trusted with his brother's life. If we must constantly be taking refuge in the walls of cities, we cannot be out working the fields.

This offense escalates, just as we saw the offense of vengeance escalating. What the United States did to nature in Southeast Asia with defoliants and herbicides, bombs and bulldozers, was unprecedented in degree. Yet the fact that nature was the victim was not a new thing. The Thirty Years' War made some of Western Europe desert for generations. The Crusades did the same thing in the Middle East. Our battleship artillery again did it to the hills behind Beirut. War always means pillage and scorched earth. The effects of a massive nuclear exchange upon our ecology will be new in degree, but we have always drawn our patient vulnerable mother earth into the suffering we inflict on our neighbors.

This is the normal extension of the curse of Cain, and specifically of the mark of Cain (the fact that he is protected by a circle of vengeance). What is destroying nature and destroying the possibility of social peace is not anarchy, but government gone beyond bounds. What is killing us is not savagery, but civilization. The saga of Genesis simply describes that fact. That is the way it is: the reciprocal interlocking of genocide and ecocide. The voice of our brothers' blood cries out to God, and we cannot live with our brother on the land. What can we do with a lost creation? What would you do? What would you try to do if you were God?

One obvious answer, the answer that most of us give most of the time, is that to save a lost creation we should do more of what God did for Cain, but do it better, do it more carefully, more effectively. We should define justice in terms of eye for eye and tooth for tooth, as did Hammurabi and Moses. We should organize as Moses did by naming judges. We should theologize it as we do with Romans 13. We should define the legitimate limits of violence as people do with the doctrine of the just war. We should verify the legitimacy of its agents, as we do with democracy. We should broaden its jurisdiction, as we try to do through the United Nations.

All of that is better than nothing, but it does not save us. It opens the door ever wider to escalation, because it absolutizes the claims it makes for itself, just as Lamech absolutized the value of revenge. When we fight a war to end war, or to make the world safe for democracy, when we destroy Vietnam to save it, when we say the Marines in Lebanon or the missiles in Wyoming are "keeping the peace," it is obvious that what is explained as a corrective or defensive measure has become itself the problem.

But then what is the alternative? What else can God do? What could you do if you were God? What could be done that would be strong enough to break the vicious cycle of vengeance?

God's other choice is to do something weak. God's ultimate choice is to work with the model of Abel.

In chapter 11 of the letter to the Hebrews, it is Abel who heads the list of believers who trusted God enough to obey him. All of those figures are people who ran risks for the sake of God's purposes. The story reflects God's priorities, to which the heroes of faith entrusted themselves. This is not an original way to read Hebrew history. Jesus already repeated an old tradition about the long lineage of holy martyrs. So the death of Jesus was not a new idea. It was not a ritual or an arbitrary decree by God dictating the requirements for our redemption. God has been working that way since the beginning of human history. Those who trusted God have always been suffering, because they counted on God and not on their power or their vengeance to assure their own future.

What is new, and what is complete in the case of Jesus, who brings this line of holy martyrs to a conclusion (Hebrews 12:2), is the proclamation, already prepared for proleptically by the holy prophets and martyrs but now confirmed by the resurrection, that that side, the Abel side, is the side that God is on. The name "Abel" to the Hebrew reader meant dust, mist, transitoriness.

That befits his fate. Yet God chooses to continue in the way of Abel. God chooses the way of weakness.

Abel was innocent, not only in the sense that he was not guilty. He was also unsuspecting, naive, harmless, ready to trust his brother. The reason for that trust was not that his brother was trustworthy. He trusted God. Thus the author of Hebrews can say (11:4c), "He died, but through his faith he is still speaking." Abel's stand is meaningful; it makes sense. It speaks because, beyond death, God is on that side. God has chosen to save the world not through the power of Cain, or through the deterrent vengeance which protected his city-building, but through the weakness of Abel.

Now we are ready to read from 1 John:

> This is the message
> as you heard it from the beginning:
> that we are to love one another;
> not to be like Cain, who belonged to the Evil One
> and cut his brother's throat simply for this reason,
> that his own life was evil and his brother lived a good life.
> You must not be surprised, brothers, when the world hates you;
> we have passed out of death and into life,
> and of this we can be sure
> because we love our brothers.
> If you refuse to love, you must remain dead;
> To hate your brother is to be a murderer,
> and murderers, as you know, do not have eternal life in them.
> This has taught us love—
> that he gave up his life for us;
> and we, too, ought to give up our lives for our brothers.
>
> *1 John 3:11-16, JB*

This text places the question of violence, killing, war, in a much wider framework than merely a teaching about right and wrong acts which might be found in a catalog of right and wrong acts. What is at stake is much more fundamental than the identity of the peace church tradition, or than the particular discussion of social values to be defended by this or that social tactic, or the debatable usefulness of certain techniques of protest or social change. What is at stake is the very identity of God, and our identity in him.

John's letter tells us that there are two models for mankind. There is Cain, whose defense is to kill, and there is Jesus, who gave his life for the brother. You can follow one or the other. Thus the list of believers that began with Abel (Hebrews 11:4) concluded with Jesus (12:2), "Who for the joy that was set before him endured the cross."

Our natural response to this is inconclusive. What does "the cross" mean? What should we do with that? What are we supposed to achieve? How can we do it well? Don't we have to figure out how it can work before we can run risks? Which risks are worth running? Isn't there such a thing as legitimate self-concern? Don't we sometimes have to stick up for ourselves? Is it possible to administer society with only the power of love? What would you do if . . . ?"

There are plenty of questions like that. The answers would have to take as many forms as the many ways in which I have just echoed the questions, if these questions were to be answered in an ecumenical debate, or in a seminary course, or in a book about theories of violence and social values. But those are not questions which the Bible writers seem to care about.

How can we be sure that it pays to do the right? How could Abel be sure? The text says, "by faith." He died a failure, an innocent victim, but "by his faith he is still speaking." The voice of a martyr's blood, we know, often speaks more strongly than that same saint did when alive.

How could Abraham be sure it was worthwhile to obey? The text says, "by faith." He left Chaldea to go God-only-knew where, and he never really got there. He was promised a great posterity. He was promised a city, which he never got to build. How could Jesus be sure? The text says, "by faith." It was "for the joy that was set before him that he endured the cross and its shame."

The biblical writers somehow did not care to know how their peace witness was going to be effective in getting a hearing, or in changing the world, or in being respectable in the eyes of the nonpacifists of their society. The biblical writers didn't take much time to clarify at just what point it should fall to us to take a costly stand against the world: whether it should be at the point of draft registration, or only that of military service, or only that of killing. Those early believers had problems of that kind. Every century has them. The answers they found then might be more help to us today than we think, but that is not the concern of Hebrews or 1 John. Their call is simply an invitation to believe, really to believe, to believe even though many others do not, to believe even though the proof is not yet final. To believe that when God acts among us he takes the side of Abel, he takes the shape of Jesus, he gives himself for others, and that that is powerful. "Anyone who comes to him must believe that he exists and rewards those who seek him."

I have been trying for a long time to understand why many peace church Christians, while not at all inclined to reject outright what in recent years we have been calling our "peace witness," are still embarrassed about saying much about it to others, feel unable to say it without being misunderstood, and want to avoid being identified too closely with those of other backgrounds who say similar things.

The good news, we say, is that God loves you and that he will forgive you, but then the bad news is that God will not love you very long if you don't love your enemy. So we have long conversations, and convene study conferences, about how to connect the good news of God's love for us with the bad news of our needing to love others: the grace with the law, Christ as gentle Savior forgiving us with Christ as imperious Lord whom we must obey. This bad joke is what we would avoid if we heard the gospel from the New Testament instead of through the filter of the American culture religion. That God was in Christ is the gospel. That God in Christ took the side of Abel, gave himself, is the gospel. That we are God's children, so that we share that nature and that self-giving activity, is our *good* news. To do so is not hard moral drudgery, nor a denominational distinctive, nor a debatable interpretation of some particular proof text about government or the taking of life. To love the neighbor, even the enemy neighbor, is itself the gift of the love of God. It is the nature of God. "We are already the children of God. What we are to be in the future is not yet been revealed; all we know is that when it is revealed we shall be like him, because we shall see him as he really is."

There remains one more step in our understanding. How do we know what we know about Abel, if he died? How do we know about Jesus, if he died? Is faith an inward phenomenon sustained in our spirit only by itself, a kind of spiritual calisthenics? Not at all! Faith is shared and supported by community; not by the world, by common sense, by the evidence of nature, but by fellow believers. Thus it is that chapter 12, which begins with the "cloud of witnesses," rises to the vision of a heavenly festival of the believers of all ages.

> What you have come to is nothing known to the senses: not a . . .
> fire or . . . darkness or a storm, or . . . thunder or . . . great
> voice. . . . What you have come to is Mount Zion and the city of
> the living God, the heavenly Jerusalem where the millions of
> angels have gathered for the festival, with the whole Church in
> which everyone is a "first-born son" and a citizen of heaven. You
> have come to God himself, the supreme Judge, and been placed
> with the spirits of saints who have been made perfect; and to Jesus,
> the mediator who brings a new covenant and a blood for purifi-
> cation which pleads more insistently than Abel's.
>
> *Hebrews 12:18-24, JB*

So we are back to the voice of the blood. The voice of our brother's blood, whom we killed, cries out against the murderer, against the oppressor. Culture is rotten at the core. Government is rotten at the core, as long as Cain flees from that pursuing voice, taking refuge in the circle of vengeance upon vengeance.

But if we can learn to see God on the side of Abel, on the side of those who are oppressed, the blacks, the Vietnamese, the Nicaraguans. . . .

If with the prophet we can see the suffering Servant of the Lord replacing David and Solomon as models for the kind of leader God wants. . . .

If with Jesus at the Jordan and in the desert we can see suffering servanthood as God's way to save Israel. . . .

If with Peter and Paul and John we can say that God did save Israel that way, that God *was* in Christ bringing the world to himself. . . .

If we can take the step from the side of Cain to that of Jesus. . . .

If we can drop our legitimate defenses as well as the other ones. . . .

Then that very same shedding of blood that was the sign of our guilt, and of the curse on the earth, and the end of trust within society, may become the sign of our redemption. The blood of our brother, of our elder brother Jesus, pleads *for* us not against us. If God in Christ loves his enemies—whom we were—if *that* is the good news, then there is no bad news. Then our loving our enemies, because we are children of God, is the gospel itself. We need only believe.

Presented at College Mennonite Church, Goshen, Indiana, June 25, 1972.

6

Glory in a Tent

The Word with God

1 In the beginning there was the Word.
    The Word was in God's presence.
  The Word was God.
2 It was present in the beginning.

The Word and Creation

3 Through it all things came to be.
  Not a thing came to be apart from it.
4 In it there was life.
  And this life was the light of men.
5 The light shines on in the dark.
  The darkness did not absorb it.
6 There came to be a man commissioned by God.
  His name was John.
7 He came for a testimony,
  To testify to the light,
    That thanks to him all would believe.
8 He was not the light
  But he was to testify to the light,
9 The true light which shines on every man
  Was coming into the world.

The Word in the World

10 He was in the world,

The world which had come to be through him,
Yet the world did not recognize him.
11 To his own he came,
        Yet his own did not accept him
12 But those who did accept him
        He empowered to become God's children.
        Those who believed in his name,
13 Engendered not in a womb,
        not by human drives,
        not by a man's decision,
        but by God.

The Word Among Us

14 Now the Word became human.
        He pitched his tent among us
   And we gazed at his glory,
        Glory abounding with enduring love,
        The glory of an only Son coming from the Father.
15 John testified to him announcing:
        This is he of whom I said:
        The one coming after me
        Has come to rank ahead of me
        Because before me, he was.
16 Of his abundance we have all received
        One grace succeeding another.
17 Now while the Law was given through Moses
        Enduring love came to be through Jesus Christ.
18 No one has ever gazed upon God.
        The only divine Son at the Father's side
        Is the one who has proclaimed him.
                                        John 1:1-18

Hardly anywhere in the Bible is the language more simple. It doesn't say anything we haven't heard before. How then shall we proceed, if we want really to hear what it says now to us?

If it were within the scope of our task to study through the text in a very careful way, literally, for all that it originally meant, one question we could not avoid struggling with is whether the lines we have before us are a poem or not. How each phrase is to be taken depends partly on what kind of literature it intends to be. The form is in favor of considering it as poetry. The lines are simple, many of them very nearly of the same length, interlocking with one another in various forms of parallelism, or in sequences where one sentence begins with the word which concluded the previous one.

If we are dealing with poetry, then it probably came into being in several stages, for there are also sections which do not have poetic form (such as 6-9, 15, 17-18 above). Then we would need to imagine two or more stages in the writing process, in which there would have existed first of all a hymn, and then some annotations on the hymn, in the course of its becoming the prologue to a Gospel. Today most scholars believe that there is some kind of poetic structure in the original author's intent, but it is not an unanimous view, and the scholars who agree that it is poetry do not agree very closely in their estimates of which lines are the oldest. So let us not claim to answer that question.

The second overall challenge to interpretation would focus on the meaning of the third section (10-12) which speaks of the light shining in the darkness and not being received. Of which time period does this speak? The first verses (1-2) have to do with before creation, the next set (3-5) with creation, and the third grouping (14f.) with the incarnation. That might lead us to think that the intervening section means to describe the history of Israel, as a long period between creation and Christ, when a light was present and continued to shine, however, never with full clarity or success.

But this third segment might also be a timeless summary, describing all of world history, including the Christian era, since it speaks of the possibility of our becoming children of God. But if that is the case, then verse 14 does not actually represent a new phase.

For our purposes we shall have to get along without settling that literary question either. Perhaps it has more than one right answer. If there were different phases in the coming into being of this text, beginning as a hymn or recitation message, used in the churches before the gospel writer incorporated it in his book, then there might have been different meanings assumed in different settings, depending on whether the hymn was being chanted in a church or written in its present context.

For our purposes we can set aside what could have been learned from that kind of analysis. We take the text as it now stands, as a coherent essay in simple rhythmic prose, an essay which serves as prologue to the rest of the Gospel book. In so doing, we lose something which could have been learned from knowing more about the composition and the structure of one line at a time, but we also gain the light that is thrown on a prologue when we know what follows.

If we don't ask any further *how* our text was written, then we should ask *why*. It is no exaggeration to say that everything in the New Testament was written against somebody. That is not said disrespectfully. That simple statement may be the best way to prepare ourselves to get the point of this particular text. Its theme is what is often called "incarnation", (becoming flesh), but that is an abstract Latin term. What it means is that God acted in a totally human way, and unhesitatingly entrusted his own cause to the hands of ordinary people. But the normal result of his presence, the logically unavoidable result of his putting himself at our mercy, is misunderstanding. We wouldn't have our New Testament if it had not been for such misunderstandings, calling forth correction, balance, and reprimand, and provoking further elaboration of what the faithful message really was.

Sometimes that corrective character of Scripture is explicit, as in some of the epistles. In other cases, as in this text, it is between the lines. If we want to know the point of a text, we must understand those alternatives which it opposes. In fact, if we really want to understand why the text needed to be written, we should be drawn to those alternatives. If we fail to see why those misunderstandings were normal or even attractive, we may fail to sense the bite of the corrective. So let us now ask what the possible misunderstandings of the meaning of incarnation were, which the author was aware of, and was seeking to ward off by the foundation he here lays for the Gospel account.

Clearly one part of the audience or the readership of this prologue was a group of people loyal to John the Baptist. The second half of John 1 is a collection of five distinct brief stories, each different in time and place and participants, but all agreeing that John the Baptist, when approached by people who wanted to know about his own mission, regularly told them to look beyond himself to Jesus, who was the one they should really be waiting for. In the two notes inserted in the text of the prologue itself (6ff., 15ff.), the same point is made in the third person in such a way that it interrupts the flow of the poetry.

Why was all that needed? Why was there any point in repeatedly telling the readers that John was not the light but only one of the witnesses to Jesus? Obviously, there must have been a body of disciples of John who took him to be the true prophet, and did not see Jesus as the fulfiller of John's promises. This surmise is supported by a few observations we could make elsewhere in the Gospels and by additional historical testimonies as well. In Acts 19, we read of disciples of John the Baptist a whole generation later in the distant city of Ephesus. A movement was still going on, somehow parallel to, and somehow in conversation with, what we usually conceive of as the early church.

It is therefore important to know what their doubt might have been. What would people have been thinking, for whom John the Baptist was himself the prophet, the light, the one the Jews had been awaiting? We know something about John's message. It was a proclamation that the kingdom of God was at hand, and a promise of judgment, which Jesus affirmed and built upon. When John found himself in prison and the kingdom had not yet come, observing that the harvest of God's righteousness had not yet been brought to the threshing floor to winnow the chaff from the grain, John sent messengers (Luke 7:18ff.) to see whether Jesus really was what John had thought was supposed to be coming. His expectations were not yet fulfilled. What Jesus had brought was not powerful enough. The Romans were still there. The collaborators were still there.

If the promise was true that God is going to act to bring righteousness, then until he has done so in the way we expected, we should not settle for anything less. The Gospel reports that Jesus told John's messengers that they should report to him that

the blind and the lame and the lepers and the deaf were being
helped. The dead were being raised, and the poor were hearing
good news. We are not told whether John's disciples considered
that to be a satisfying answer. Nor are we told what John himself
thought when the message reached him—if it did.

When Jesus later suffered the "defeat" of his crucifixion,
there was all the more reason for the disciples of John to conclude
that Jesus was not the awaited one. It is better to keep waiting
than to lower our sights. It is better to believe that God is really
going to bring justice, just not so soon, than to be satisfied with
something less than divine victory. The victory of Jesus was not
dramatic enough. The defeat of God's enemies was not real
enough. The Christian movement was too modest, and too dependent upon faith—not definite enough, not proven. In the
great heritage of prophetic promise of which their leader John had
been (as Jesus agreed) a worthy culmination, there were good
reasons to expect something more, something bigger and less am-
biguous, less dependent upon faith, and less persecuted.

So it is not just a necessary bridge in the narrative between a
timeless introduction and a subsequent narrative, when John
points away from himself to Jesus. It is a serious debate at the
portal of the early church. The writer is affirming, in a situation
where that is by no means something to be taken for granted, that
what came in Jesus is really what the Baptist wanted, and that was
not easy to believe.

How many of us recognize ourselves in the disciples of John?
Maybe we first came to care about peace as a righteous cause.
Maybe somebody told us that righteousness had to triumph, and
that things were so bad there had to be a turning point. And then
the turning point did not come. The campuses cooled, the war
was declared a victory and continued under another name. Feed-
ing the hungry yesterday just prepares more people to starve
tomorrow. Why should we stand up for the right if God doesn't?
It made sense to sing, "Conquer we must, for our cause it is just;
this is our motto, in God is our trust," when victory was assured.
But why should we trust him if we will not conquer?

Or perhaps we are disciples of John in another sense. Perhaps the victory we think God owes us is experiential. We want it proven to us, through some undebatable, undeniable experience, that God is real and is on our side. An exorcism perhaps, or a vision, a voice, or a miracle. Then we need to be reminded that revelation comes among us in a form that we can choose to reject.

Another kind of opposition also shows in the context of our passage, although literally it is visible only on the edges. In the Gospel proper (which thereby throws light on the prologue), there is constant pressure on Jesus from the political and religious establishment. The Gospel sometimes refers to these people as "high priests" or as "chief priests and Pharisees," sometimes more simply as "the Jews," or perhaps more accurately "the Judeans." This does not mean all the Jews as such—the common folk, the people of the land, the man in the street, the silent majority. It means what we today refer to with the slogan expression, "the establishment." It means those people who understood their sacred duty to be the institutional defense and preservation of the heritage of Scripture and tradition as received from their fathers. They understood Jesus to be rejecting this heritage, because he was challenging their own faithfulness to it.

Jesus claimed only to be fulfilling the meaning of that tradition, and we can confirm that claim as we read the documents of the Jewish tradition. But they, the establishment ("the Jews" in that sense), thought he was a rebel against that tradition and a threat to it. It is tragic how often and how long Christians have agreed with Caiaphas and Annas that Jesus is anti-Jewish, or that the early Christians were anti-Jewish. This is simply not true. But it is true that Christianity sees itself as going beyond Moses. It sees in Jesus one grace succeeding the one which had gone before (v. 16, "one grace succeeding another"). It sees promise fulfilled and expectation confirmed in the way in which Jesus leads God's people beyond where the earlier prophets had led them, but still in the same direction.

Even in his conflict with the establishment, Jesus was part of the Jewish tradition. The expressions "the light shines in the dark-

ness while the darkness does not receive it'" (v. 5) and "he came
to his own but his own did not receive him" (v. 11) may in some
other context have meant very broadly that truth comes to humanity or that revelation has sought in many times and places to
break through to all people. But in the present context we
probably do well to understand them as referring to the Hebrew
story, when the speaking of God through the centuries was addressed in a very special way to the children of Abraham and to
the people of Moses, who, however, as a whole did not hear and
obey.

There is a pattern in the Old Testament story like that which
we are about to observe in the Gospel of John. God's Word coming to his own and not being received by them is not a new event
when it happens in the career of Jesus. It had always been that
way with the prophets, a point which Jesus himself makes
elsewhere in the Gospel stories. Are we at all tempted by that posture, which closes off God's acting now, on the grounds that we
know for sure he spoke in the past?

At only one point in the above text have I followed a
somewhat original rendering: the phrase "enduring love" (v. 14)
stands where the Greek has literally "grace and truth." Here I am
following one of the most complete and competent recent in-
terpreters, Raymond E. Brown, author of the *Anchor Bible* com-
mentary. One noun after another is the simplest way to state in
Hebrew what we would state in English with a noun and an ad-
juective. Grace and truth are not two separate realities, but two
ways of describing one reality. In Hebrew you say it with a phrase
like "enduring love" or "loving faithfulness".

Incidentally, this is one of the points at which the vocabulary
of the prologue is distinct from the rest of the Gospel. "Grace" is a
common term in Paul but not in John. "Truth" is an extremely
important concept in John's Gospel. In fact it is one of the names
Jesus claims for himself. But precisely therein it has a different
meaning from that of this specific passage.

The designation of "Law" and of "Moses," as the earlier
covenant which has now been surpassed, is also not quite the lan-

guage of the rest of John's Gospel. It is more like the writings of Paul. The claim is not that what was known in Moses and the law was something other than enduring love. The claim is that enduring love could not be gazed upon in its fullness ("fullness" is another word more frequent in Paul than in John) because it had not yet "come to be"; it had not yet entered into our own condition.

Our author has yet another adversary group or position. We do not know whether these people were organized, or what they called themselves. They are never named as a party in the New Testament, but their position is present, and what they thought is clear. They deny the point which is affirmed so bluntly in verse 14 of our prologue, that the word became flesh, that the message of God became tangible in fully human form.

In the first letter of John, we find the label "false prophets" used for people who deny that Jesus Christ came in the flesh. Elsewhere that same book uses the label "antichrist" for those who deny Jesus Christ. But let us be careful not to misunderstand. To deny Jesus Christ today would mean being a secularist, an agnostic, or an atheist, claiming in one way or another that there is not, or that there is no way to talk about, a transcendent reality coming to us in Jesus. The doubters in the late first century were making just the opposite point. They did know about transcendent reality. They thought of themselves precisely as the knowing ones. They saw themselves as responsible for the preservation and refinement of a high level of religious insight. Historians call their position "gnostic," from a root which refers to special inside knowledge. They were the insightful, the initiated. Today we might call them gurus, maharishis, or systematic theologians.

The special knowledge these people were concerned about was the reality of God himself, which they were profoundly concerned to safeguard against dilution and pollution and any admixture with the human. To be divine is to be different. It is the differentness of God which we therefore must safeguard. To be more divine is to be different and most distant. The real sub-

ject matter of belief is that distant God himself. From that
perspective, then, Jesus is too close to us and too simple, too accessible, too impermanent.

If God is most adequately conceived of in his unity, distance,
and purity, then the only way from him to us would have to be a
very long ladder. The name for that ladder, at least for some of
the gnostics, was precisely the term we have here: the WORD.
Our gospel uses the technical term *Logos*, WORD, which the
gnostics used to describe that mediating principle which could
reach down across the numerous steps and stages from God to us.
The WORD for them was not the same as either God himself or
man himself but rather the ladder between the two funda-
mentally incomparable and incompatible levels. So when they
denied that God could be touched in the flesh, this was not doubt,
but piety; not unbelief, but high spirituality.

For this very logical understanding of communication, the
difference between a word and the speaker is evident. When you
speak to your neighbor, your word is an indispensable vehicle of
who you are and what you mean to say, but it is not the same as
yourself. All the words you can think of to say will not exhaust
who you are, and some of them may actually confuse or mislead.
So for the gnostic, the WORD is the first and most elevated of the
creatures of God, yet still only a creature.

How did John answer this overly religious orientation? One
way to avoid a heresy is to avoid its language and to avoid contact
with that kind of people. One avoids even the hint of an echo of
the false teaching by proscribing wrong vocabulary, by forbidding
heretical expressions.

But here in our prologue, the approach is the reverse. The
key concept of the gnostic vision of the link between God and
man, namely the WORD, is adopted and used to make the opposite point. At the one end of the bridge, the word is identified
with us, with flesh, with the finite, the historical, the present.
What the gnostics were afraid of, for fear that the power and
reality of divinity would be dulled, the Gospel now affirms is
precisely what has happened, not in mankind as a whole but in

Jesus in particular. In order to say that, our author has, so to speak, requisitioned the intellectual property of the adversary. He takes terms which were meant to safeguard against a too concrete presence of God, and uses them to affirm that presence.

Perhaps the original outline of the poem might have existed before. If we look carefully at the middle section of the poem, it could have been a pre-Christian text. It could be a general description of the human predicament, as surrounded by darkness into which the light penetrates only seldom and uncertainly. It could be read as a document of the predicament of truth, which when it comes to its own is not received.

In that way, standing alone, the middle section of the original poem could have been a gnostic hymn, a lamentation on the darkness of the world. I make that suggestion not because there is any textual evidence that a part of our text once existed as a gnostic hymn, but because the very idea illustrates the radical risk taken by a missionary strategy which adopts the language of its challengers as the instrument of its own witness.

John Frederic Oberlin, a pietist country pastor two centuries ago in a lonely valley between Alsace and the rest of France, father of the kindergarten and of agricultural extension, for whom in the next century a college in Ohio was named, was in the middle of his career when the French Revolution did away with religion. Public Christian worship was prohibited, to be replaced by the adoration of the goddess Reason. All over France the people were commanded to gather on July 14 to hear patriotic discourses about liberty, equality, and fraternity and speeches against all tyrants. Without missing a step Oberlin rose before his villagers on Bastille Day and preached about Christian liberty, Christian equality, Christian brotherhood, and against the tyranny of hatred and avarice.

The sample is superficial but the strategy is radical. It is not without serious dangers. We can sense some of them when today we pick up the challenge of paraphrasing the name of Christ in terms of liberation, or self-fulfillment, or meaningful relationships, or being for others. The danger is that we may adopt the language of our doubting audience in order to say what they want to hear. The test of faithfulness will be whether we can use the language of the crowd or the fad to say just the opposite.

That is what the Gospel prologue does with the language of gnosticism. It turns inside out a whole system of thought, whose entire purpose had been to dramatize the distance between the spirituality of God and our poor humanity, and to describe the need for rare and costly exercises of meditation and initiation to seek to rise in contemplation just a step or two toward that distant light. This is the language which is seized and stood on its head to claim—no to proclaim—that all of the meaning behind creation, all of the orderliness and purposefulness and goal-directedness of the created order, has come right into our life in a form which preposterously puts itself at our mercy, letting it depend on us whether we will let it illuminate us, transform us, and make us children of God.

If you didn't recognize yourself among the disciples of John, or among the defensive establishment, maybe you belong here. Perhaps you recognize yourself among the seekers after wisdom and deeper insight. Can it be glory if it comes to us in a tent? Can it be the Lord God if it comes to us as a human? Can it be real if it happened centuries ago? Is our faith not supposed to pull us up out of the transitory, the uncertain, and the unsure to set us on another level? Don't we have to think things through more deeply? If that is our search—it is especially often the search of the student—then we do need to be told again that there is another level of truth all right, but that it came to us.

We have located the text in terms of its adversaries; now what does it say?

Nothing of what this text says is unheard of to us. Yet it is over and over again what we need to hear. The distortions against which it warns are still our old temptations. Do we not still really think that when there is a revelation it must be powerful, unambiguous, undeniable? Yet it was the fate of that revelation of the Word to be rejected, and that not by those who were inherently his enemies but *by his own.* He came to his own. He came where he had a right to expect acceptance, and it was his own people who did not hear. This has been happening ever since Adam, ever since Abraham, ever since Moses. Since Jesus it still happens, that the depth of the suffering of God is not the blunt and brutal rebelliousness of the reprobate, but the refusal of his own to receive him.

We have good reason to look separately at these three distinct challenges to which the prologue is addressed. Sometimes we ourselves are like the disciples of John. We want a symbol of power that proves itself to us, without a need for faith, by its own overwhelming impact. Sometimes like the Judean establishment we want to make the truth accountable to our need for security. Often, like the gnostics, we long for a religious reality to pull us away from ourselves and from the simplicity and reality of "the flesh."

The simplicity of the gospel story embarrasses us in all three directions. For us, as for the disciples of John, it is weakness. For us, as for the spiritual elite, it is disconcerting by the fact of being physical, local, and temporal. For the "establishment" in us all it is shallow, contemporary, and changing.

But for now let us rather generalize beyond all three. We may observe that what they have in common, in their several forms, is an impatience with the reality of our life within the limits of creation and history. To appeal to the power of liberation from on high, to appeal to the dignity of revelation from on high, or to take refuge in the authority of a tradition once received, are all ways of stepping back from the risk of the present reality to a basic unbelief. In response to that common attraction, this text, like a few others elsewhere in the New Testament, says two apparently contradictory things.

It says first that what has come among us in the word and work of Jesus is far more than the word and work of a man, since what it brings us has the dignity of preexistence, of having shared in the divine work of creation. That the world is created, or that God is Creator, was not a new idea and was not significant information to a Jewish Christian reader when this passage said it.

But that that which comes to us in Jesus is no different from the truth and the power of creation is a new claim. It is in fact a claim which, in a systematic way, most theologies to our day do not really believe.

Most theologies distinguish in some deep way between creation and redemption. For example, according to Martin Luther in classical Protestantism, or Emil Brunner or H. Richard Niebuhr in recent times, creation and redemption have two different sets of ethical implications. If you derive your value system from creation, you will, for instance, defend the state, which is an institution of creation. If you derive your guidance from redemption alone, then the teachings and the example of Jesus can be normative for you, which may lead to nonresistance. But you only have the right to draw nonresistant conclusions from the teachings of Jesus if you admit that the realm of creation is governed by other laws and other authorities. In other words, Jesus speaks for God all right, as did the prophets before him, but God also has other distinct channels through which he has said other distinct things, which we may perceive by using other modes of hearing God, such as the reasonable analysis of the Word that is in creation.

It is thus not simply a speculative difference, but a very concrete one, when the apostolic generation responsible for this text and its parallels insisted that what is known in Jesus is precisely the same, in authority and in meaning, as what underlies creation. When he says "there was nothing of what came to be that did not come to be through him," John is not propounding a new theory about creation. He is simply repeating the Genesis report, which shows God creating by his Word. But from that report he draws a negation. God has not revealed himself otherwise. He has not revealed a different purpose or character through creation than what we now encounter through Jesus.

This insistence is by no means peculiar to the text we are reading. There are other texts in the New Testament, written by other authors to other readers, which in a quite parallel way accentuate the claim that what is known in Jesus is what was behind creation. Let us listen to the letter *to the Hebrews* (1:1-3):

In many and various ways God spoke of old to our fathers by the prophets; but in these last days he has spoken to us by a son, whom he appointed the heir of all things, through whom also he created the world.

Or shall we hear Colossians (1:15-17):

He is the image of the invisible God, the firstborn of all creation; for in him all things were created. . . . He is before all things, and in him all things hold together.

The same claim is made in fewer words in the early Christian hymn which the apostle Paul quotes in Philippians 2, which without specific reference to creation speaks of the Son having been in the form of God and of equality with God as being within his grasp, prior to his "emptying" himself.

This is more than the doubters of the humanity of Jesus would have asked. The disciples of John would have been satisfied with another Elijah. The chief priests and Pharisees would have accepted another Moses or another David. But our author is not interested in satisfying critics; he is singing praises.

But more powerful and more original is the thrust in the other direction. Our own author and the parallel passages written to the Hebrews, Colossians, and Philippians make the same point. The way the Creator WORD came among us was not in dignity and effectiveness but in weaknesses, suffering, and defeat. *The Word became flesh and lived in a tent among us.* That the WORD became flesh does not mean merely that he came within our reach, that he became visible—not only that he translated himself into terms which we could grasp. For that, it would have been enough to speak once more in prophetic word as he had done before. Or it would have been enough to speak in a perfect book like the Quran of Islam. Or it would have been enough to give his authorization to a powerful human institution like the Sanhedrin or the Vatican. The choice of "flesh" to describe his dwelling among us, like the choice of the verb "to dwell in a tent," does not mean simply that God became tangible. It means he became weak, undignified, vulnerable. The power behind creation came among us in such a way that we can hurt him.

That is then the core of the message of the prologue. The weakness of the flesh is not a contradiction of the claims which John is making for Jesus. It is precisely his acceptance of weakness and unworthiness that is the measure of his love, because that is where we are. How much did God love the world? So much that he gave his only son. The quantitative accent of our text, if we read one phrase at a time ("unique son in the bosom of the Father," "with God from the beginning") is on the glory and dignity of the WORD. But that is not new information for any serious Jew, messianic or not, who might have heard that hymn or read that Gospel. The qualitative accent is on the tent, all the more noticeable because in the rest of the Gospel Jesus is compared not with the tabernacle but with the temple.

Let us try to think ourselves back into the minds of Christians of the second or third generation. Christians of that time, as they gathered around the apostles whose memories of Jesus were firsthand and vibrant, knew about the cross because they knew very well the place it happened and could understand how it happened and what it meant. For them it was enough, to be both meaningful and convincing, that they should hear that story told with the authority of the eyewitness. For the first-generation Jewish Christian to see that as a story of obedience, on which God had placed his blessing by the resurrection, was all it took to make sense.

But now we are a generation or two later. We are outside of Palestine. We don't know intimately an apostle who really saw it all happen. We don't know the places, or the Jewish culture. Then the very simplicity and concreteness and realism of the Gospel story, which had been advantages in the beginning ,become handicaps. An apostolic report can be forgotten or contested. A communal memory can grow dim or be reinterpreted or seem strange. That one event way back there is so specific and so local. Can we really go on celebrating it as the hinge of history?

It is to this that the authors or the poets behind the high points of the New Testament witness respond when they proclaim that what happened in the cross is a revelation of the shape of what God is, and of what God does, in the total drama of history. They affirm as a permanent pattern what in Jesus was a particular event. The eternal WORD condescending to put himself at our mercy, the creative power behind the universe emptying itself, pouring itself into the frail mold of humanity, has the same shape as Jesus. God has the same shape as Jesus, and he always has had. The cross is what creation is all about. What Jesus did was local, of course, because that is how serious and real our history is to God. But what the cross was locally is universally and always the divine nature.

Ordinary religious philosophy begins by knowing, on its own grounds, what God must be like, and then stretches and twists to affirm that somehow Jesus is uniquely like that. These texts reverse that. They look at Jesus and confess that God is like him.

Later theological discussion will be dominated by the philosophical question, "How can God become man? How can the infinite become finite?" "Incarnation" becomes the technical label for this. For centuries, the fact that God accomplished the philosophically impossible was a dominant theme of theology, making this passage a key to extremely complicated debates around the logical puzzles of how to fit a miracle into careful human language. Definitions of just how to describe the Trinity in the fourth century, or just how to refer to the two natures of Christ in the fifth century, dramatized the centrality of this text and of the idea that the WORD's crossing the line between the divine and human levels of reality was what saved us.

Then in early modern times that same logical impossibility, which for a millennium and a half had been the dramatic symbol of salvation, became a central stumbling block. The mood in which our culture can think about transcendence (about ultimate realities on another level from what is immediately visible) has changed. Now, to say these things about the WORD as part of the divine nature, or about the divine WORD becoming one human being, must in the minds of many be meaningless by definition. So the passage which used to dramatize the center of the faith is now a barrier to belief. Every few years a theological best-seller wiggles its way through a new sequence of redefinitions and explanations, trying to help the readers to believe something without being put off by the language.

All of that is important to discuss for its own sake, but it can lead us away from what the passage meant to say. The author of these lines did not intend to draw our attention to a logical puzzle. He did not want his readers to be put off by the logical impossibility of what he is saying. And it is just as dubious that he wanted them, like early medieval theology, to be turned on by its impossibility, its miraculousness. For him there was nothing unthinkable about there being in the divine nature a second something like the WORD which is at the same time within God himself and yet distinct in such a way as to reach toward men.

The WORD, you remember, is not the Bible. It is not even Jesus—yet. The paraphrase above properly translates "it" in verses 1-5, and could properly continue that way yet in 10-12. The Word is a facet, an aspect of God himself: God-seen-as-self-imparting, God-as-communicating.

Even the thoroughly monotheistic Jews had been speaking for centuries in terms like that about what they called "wisdom" (Prov. 1:20-29; 3:13-20; 8:22-30). Nor could it be for the Gospel writer a philosophical puzzle that God should choose to, or should be able to, become flesh if he wished. To develop a massive argumentation around the miraculousness of God doing what by the nature of things he could not do is therefore to misunderstand the heart of our passage, whether you do it reverently as the Middle Ages did, or with embarrassment like much modern theology.

Our author is not attracted by doubts about whether what he says happened could have happened. The text is not a theological discussion at all. It is a "testimony," as it says. A testimony is a particular kind of human communication. It involves the speaker more than some kinds of communication do, because it must say "I have seen" or "we have heard." That is what this passage does in verse 14 and again in verse 16. But as distinct from much personal communication, especially in our modern cultures which have trained us to be very self-conscious, and as distinct from modern pietism, *testimony* is not language which talks about oneself, except as a beholder or a listener. To be a witness is to point to something beyond oneself—something that was there, that others could have seen or heard or touched in the same way, if they had been there.

The normal usage of the word "witness" is in the courtroom. Its purpose there is to lead the judges or the jury to understand and to believe the objective reality of what the witness reports. So John's purpose is not to dramatize incarnation as a miracle, heightening the religiousness of faith by dramatizing its unlikelihood. He is only interested in directing our attention to the fact of God's having chosen to make himself heard and his having been heard, not in another thundercloud as at Sinai and not in just one more prophet, but in the tangible humanness of a man among men.

Perhaps this point can be clarified with a feeble modern example. In recent years, we have not known quite what to do about the reports of people who say that they observed objects in the sky which by their shape or their behavior could not have been man-made aircraft. A label has even been coined, which is really a nonterm, "unidentified flying object." It is rumored that one person was especially clear that one of those was what she had seen, because it had the letters UFO painted on the side.

Now what interferes with our believing these reports is our knowledge, or more precisely our convictions substantiated by considerable cultural experience, and by scientific theories and engineering rules, that things like that just don't happen. Our skepticism is further supported by information about optical illusions, and psychologically generated hallucinations, and suggestion, and other ways people can fool themselves. So when we hear another report that someone has definitely identified as an unidentified flying object something they saw, there are two not fully compatible processes going on in our mind. One is the struggle with our definitions, which doubt the possibility of such a thing, and the other is the normal procedure that we follow when listening to anyone who claims to have seen something and wants us to believe it was there—listening to a witness.

Now if we want to understand what John is trying to tell us about Jesus, we must move our minds from the first kind of question to the second. He is not trying to say anything about whether it is possible that the impossible has happened. He is rather testifying that what God always was continues. And what the WORD of God was always trying to do in creation and in the garden of Eden and in Abraham and in Moses and in the prophets—shining on faithfully even though the darkness did not receive it—continues. That same revelatory thrust within the very nature of God has now reached its culmination. One grace has succeeded another. Enduring love, which was always there, could now be beheld in its fulfillment. That this has happened is not a puzzle at all. It is the way it had to be, if God is the God he always was—the God of enduring love.

What John wants to tell us about is not that the puzzle of whether it could happen has been resolved by a miracle. What he wants to tell us is how it happened. That it happened through a man. Through an ordinary man, a Jewish man, a poor man, a man who spoke with authority and yet as a servant. A man who gave himself for his disciples instead of solving the world's problems by pushing people around. Through that completely real but very distinctive humanity, the possibility given to us to become children of God has been more clearly defined.

We now know what it means to become children of God because we have seen one. It has been guaranteed that we can be children of God because there has been one. That is the glory our author has seen, and into which he wants his readers to be ready to be swept along, as they now follow the pointing figure of the Baptist who says "that is the one we were waiting for," "there is the Lamb," and as they enter into the narrative of the rest of the Gospel to encounter again and again (2:11; 12:23f.; 13:31; 17:2ff; 22ff.) the story of the glory the author has already seen.

Festival of the Word, Goshen College, Goshen, Indiana. April 19, 1974.

7

The Form of a Servant?

The New Testament does not have a psalter. The poetry of the early Christians can only be found embedded in other texts, recognizable by the traces of rhyme or rhythm. Only seldom are these embedded quotations long enough to give us an idea of the drift of the poem as a whole. Fortunately, the longest text of such a poem that we do have in the New Testament is also probably the oldest. It was in use as a hymn in the churches before the letter to the Philippians was written.

Linguists agree, on grounds of style and rhythm, that the seven verses we are looking at were a hymn. They are not original words of the apostle Paul. He wove them into his letter, as a preacher or letter-writer may do with poetry today. Let's first of all remind ourselves of the words:

> Christ Jesus, being in the form of God,
> did not cling to his equality with God,
> but emptied himself, taking the form of a slave.
> Bearing the human likeness,
> revealed in human shape,
> he humbled himself, in obedience accepting death,
>   even death on a cross.
> Therefore God has raised him to the highest

and bestowed on him the name above all names,
that at the name of Jesus every knee should bow
     in heaven, on earth, and in the depths,
And every tongue confess, to the glory of God the Father,
     that JESUS CHRIST IS LORD.

Philippians 2:5-11

Paul weaves this quotation into his own appeal to the believers at Philippi to be more united. Even his own language here is more rhetorical, and more careful than usual. Even Paul almost rhymes:

> . . . Is there any consolation in Christ?
> . . . Is there any incentive in love?

But for now we want to look at the hymn text. It needs to be read on five levels. First of all, we need to ask, How is it a description of what Jesus did? What did Jesus do that fits this description? Jesus made a right choice, it says, when there was a wrong choice he might have made. What would the wrong choice have been? But that, we discover, is a question on the second level. There is a ground floor or a basement level before that. We must first ask who it could have been who did wrongly consider equality with God as something to grasp. The reference is to Genesis.

"Being in God's likeness" does not, here in this text, mean being God. Eve and Adam were made in God's image and likeness. To be in the likeness of God is to be human. The tempter's offer in Genesis 3:5 was godlikeness, as if it were something which Eve and Adam did not already possess. The tempter claimed that God was keeping something from them—something they could seize. Instead of accepting the godlikeness they already had as a gift, Eve and Adam believed it was a prize they could grasp. That is the ground floor, the root act of rebellion.

Now when did Jesus make a choice like that, but opposite to it? He met the same tempter. He met him not in a garden at first, but in a desert. Jesus' choice was also about godlikeness. The tempter said to him, "If you are God's Son, do this in order to claim your kingdom. Make bread. Leap into the temple court. Make a Faustian deal with me." When the tempter said, "If you are God's Son," that did not mean "If you are the second person of the Trinity," any more than it had meant that in Genesis. It meant far more concretely, humanly, politically, "If you are the anointed one, if you are the awaited liberator, if you are the one designated to rule these people and to free them, *then* do these things I offer you."

In the original setting of Psalm 2, the text which the heavenly voice had echoed at the baptism of Jesus, a priest or prophet spoke on God's behalf to the king being installed on David's throne. He said: "You are my son: this day I have begotten you" (that is, "I have adopted you as my son"). That meant, "You are now king of Israel."

So the devil says, "If that is who you are, if you are the one designated for kingship, then seize power! Take over! I can help you. These kingdoms are mine to give." That is what Jesus chose not to do. He chose in the desert not to do it. He chose again in Galilee and again in Gethsemane not to do it. His way to be the anointed one was to be not the ruler but the servant—to empty himself. His way to be godlike was human-like.

Jesus made that choice not once but over and over. He refused in the desert to be a Che Guevara or a George Washington. Instead, he held people's children, in an age before Pampers. He washed people's dirty feet. He healed their hemorrhages. He forgave their sins. He refused again at the end, in the garden, to be a George Washington or a Che Guevara. He remained the servant all the way to his death.

It may be Paul who added to the text the phrase, which doesn't fit the rhythm of the hymn, "even the death of the cross." Not any old death. He didn't die of illness, old age, or hunger, or accident. It was a political death—death on a cross, the death which the Romans reserved for rebels. That is why he is rewarded. He is given a title he didn't have before. He is now to be called "Lord," the title above all others. "Therefore," the last section begins—on the grounds of the self-abasement—the exaltation, the unique title, "Lord" was awarded him.

The most nearly parallel text elsewhere in the New Testament is Hebrews 12. There Jesus is in the same way bound to us, sharing our humanness as his way to be the divine Word. He is "the author of our faithfulness" and "the one who brings it to perfection." There Jesus is in the same way rewarded for his humiliation. The Hebrews text says that "it was for the joy that was set before him that he endured the cross." Thus the path of the cross is not an accident. It is not a detour on the way to victory. It is the victory. It is not the bitter that we have to take with the sweet. It is not the law that comes before the gospel. It is not the bad news mixed with the good. It *is* the good news. Divine self-emptying *is* the gospel. It is the revelation of the way things are.

When we read such texts about suffering, our concern is often with the dimension of pain, division, judgment, and punishment in the message of the cross. That is our agenda. That is what we are worried about. We don't want Jesus to divide us. We don't want a divine parent to chastise us. We don't want to have to take on the thankless role of judges or dividers. We would want an unbroken world. We would want a benevolent cosmos, an extension of the womb's security. So these texts bother us with their word of suffering and division. But that isn't the tone of the texts. They talk of a context of joy—"the joy that was set before him." Jesus even talks (Mark 10:29-30) about the divided family as made up for one hundredfold by finding a new family, even in this world.

The first level of our text was the human choices (wrong ones) of our first parents. The second level was the right human choices of the man Jesus. Now we move to the third level. What did this hymn mean at Philippi? What did it mean to the missionary churches of the first century? The Gentile churches were no longer in touch with the Jewish world of the Gospel narratives. They were no longer in touch with Hebrew language, where even Adam or Israelite kings would be spoken of as godlike, as "son of God." The apostolic missionaries were newly in touch with the

Hellenistic cultural world, with its concern for the material, the eternal, the "ultimately real." In that frame, the texts soon took on another meaning.

Now the phrase "he was in the form of God" came to mean the eternal preexistence of the divine Word, the second person of the Trinity. The option which he chose and carried out was then to renounce divine prerogatives, to come down to earth, and to be made man for our salvation. The hymn itself does not say that. It says nothing about coming down from heaven, but our creeds do. With the creeds ringing in our ears, we cannot help hearing that being said in this text. So the decision of Jesus not to be a violent zealot Messiah now comes to be seen as the surfacing, the manifestation, the incarnation of the deep reality of God's own nature.

You see the shape or color of a rock stratum where it sticks out of the hillside, but you know it reaches all the way back into the hill that way, maybe for miles. As you see the grain of a piece of wood at its edges, Jesus' choice not to rule the world violently is now seen to be the surfacing of an eternal divine decision (if there can be such a thing as an eternal decision)—an eternally binding and freeing decision of the Son, very God of very God, to enter into our history. Then self-emptying is not only what Jesus did. It is not only what the eternal divine Son did. If it is that, then it is the very nature of God. The Creator of the universe is a servant. The Almighty loves his enemies.

After all that glory, the fourth level of meaning seems to us to be quite a comedown, and yet it is the first level in the order of writing. Paul has colossal nerve, arrogance almost (in French we would call it *le culot*, in Yiddish, *chutzpa*). He has such a poor sense of proportion that he appeals to the heroic wrestling of Jesus with temptation in the desert. Or he even appeals to the eternal divine decree which before all worlds committed the God of the galaxies to Bethlehem and Calvary. Paul has the presumptuousness to tell the people in Philippi that that is why they ought to get along better together. This entire majestic hymn of cosmic salvation and epic Christology was preserved for us only because

Paul was pastorally pleading, from his prison, with some leadership people at Philippi, not to be so petty and proud. This means concretely the people in 1:15 who were preaching Christ out of envy or rivalry. It means concretely the two women ministers in 4:2 whom he entreats to work together better. It includes Paul's gratitude (4:10ff.) for the money they had sent him. So human, so material is the meaning for Philippi of the cosmic condescension of the eternal Son. That is the meaning of the mindedness of Jesus. That is the shape of a God who chooses servanthood. It cashes out so simply: "Do nothing from selfishness or vanity. Count others better than yourself. Look to the interests of others." Could it be more simple or more total?

The fifth level is for us to define. We gather from among the number of those who have convenanted to honor these ancient writings and this ancient hymn as holy Scripture. That time-bound text, written by Paul from some prison—Ephesus in the year 55 or Caesarea in 59 or in Rome in 62—we don't even know which, he was in prison so often—to a handful of believers in the provincial trade center of Philippi. This text is supposed to be for us, a word of grace.

Our choice is after all, he tells us, the same as the one Jesus faced, the one Eve faced. Will we reach out for dignity, importance, achievement, for godlikeness as a thing to grasp and to hold? Will we grab for sovereignty in the small world we can control? Or might we learn to trust that our worthiness as bearers of God's image was given us, so that we need not grab it? Given us, in fact, to be passed on, to be given further?

The originality of modern peacemakers like Gandhi and King was not just in their own moral character, or their shrewd sense of timing, or their spiritual discipline. It was also, centrally, in their commitment to the dignity of the adversary—the enemy. Even the oppressor is a bearer of God's image. To be bearer of the image is not a merit, not an achievement, nor something to be grasped. It is God' grace. I can then not accept that grace for myself if I fail to put my neighbor, even my enemy, in the same light.

We live in a culture in which even secular social science analysis is beginning to label self-concern, narcissism, the appetite for esteem, as one cause of our loss of social fiber. Might Paul's presumptuousness break through as good news to us? Can the ancient hymn help us to let godlikeness, dignity, self-respect be redefined as not achievement, but gift? Not dominion but servanthood?

> In the name of the Author of our faithfulness,
> in the name of the one who brings our faithfulness to perfection,
> in the name of him who for the joy that was set before him,
>   endured the shame,
> May the God of peace,
> who brought again from the dead our Lord Jesus,
>   the Great Shepherd of our flock,
> equip us, by the blood of the eternal covenant,
> to do his will in everything good,
> working in us what is pleasing in his sight
> through Jesus Christ,
> to whom be glory for ever and ever and ever,
> Amen.

Given as a vesper homily at Holden Village in Chelan, Washington, on August 24, 1983.

8

The Hilltop City

We want to turn our minds to a master image of the prophetic literature of the Hebrew Bible, an image which occurs in more than one text, looking closest at what that image means in Isaiah, Micah, and Zechariah, but without forgetting its parallels in the books of Ezekiel and Revelation.

The city of God on a hill is sometimes (as in Isaiah, Micah, Zechariah) elevated above the other hills (which look down on Jerusalem from all about today as they did then) by some kind of geological miracle.

In Revelation, on the other hand, this city comes down from heaven, and yet is still somehow parallel to Jerusalem and Mt. Zion.

Often (as in Ezekiel, Zechariah, and Revelation) the city is a source of water flowing both to east and west, giving life to trees and fields in its path.

That recurrent prophetic picture has something perennial to tell us about the purposes of God in and for the world. I want to attempt only to paraphrase or to translate it, suggesting only tentatively where it fits in our agenda. We look first at the text as we find it in Zechariah:

When that day comes,
　There will be no more cold,
　　no more frost;
It will be a day of wonder,
　with no alternation of day and night.
Running waters will issue from Jerusalem;
　half of them to the Eastern Sea,
　half of them to the Western Sea.
　They will flow summer and winter,
and Yahweh will be the king of the whole world.
Jerusalem will be raised higher,
　though still in the same place:
Jerusalem will be safe to live in.

The goal of God at the end of history is building a city—a civilizing process. The story began with a man and a woman alone in a garden. It began again with Noah landing on a mountain on the far northeastern edge of the world. It began again on the stormy peak of Sinai on the southern edge of the world. But it will come to its triumphant conclusion in a city: a garden city, set on a hill for all to see, right in the middle of the world. Because God is in the midst of the city, no lamps are needed and (except in Ezekiel) no temple. All the nations will come to it to bring tribute and to learn.

This means (secondly) that the purpose of God is a *teaching* process—reaching all the nations.

It is described in legal terms:

Out of Zion shall go forth law;
He shall judge . . .
He shall decide . . .

But this "judgment" does not mean punishment or prosecution. It means establishing a right order.

We note that the nations do not become Israelites. It is not said that they change their diet. There is no mention of circumcision or even of sacrifice. They come to learn the law of the Lord. They come voluntarily.

As Micah has it:

Nations without number . . . will say:

> "Come let us pilgrimage
>   to the mountain of Yahweh,
>   to the house of God of Jacob;
> that he may teach us his ways
> and we may walk in his paths."

The first meaning of "civilize," the linguistic root meaning of the word, is the building of a city. The ordinary meaning of the verb, however, is the transfer of knowledge. To civilize is to educate someone. That knowledge in this case is moral knowledge. It is called a "way." The nations will not know that way except by learning it. They do not know it by nature.

Before we go on, we could take note of some of the issues that arise from the text for us.

Is there something about peacemaking paths today that has to be learned? That has to be learned from Jerusalem? Can it be learned without joining the Jerusalem religion?

In our jargon, "Can the message of peace reach further than faith in the gospel?"

In the contemporary peace movement issues of that shape surface in several places. We have seen the debate about whether the Strategic Arms Limitation Treaty (SALT) was a positive step, although inadequate, or worse than nothing. We have seen the debate about a freeze without abolition or about abolishing "nukes" without abolishing war. We have seen the reminders that an antiarmament position based on fear for one's own survival is hardly as morally valid as one based on Christian love.

All of these are a part of the picture if we start believing that the peace of the prophets' proclamation, while centering in Jerusalem, should draw all the nations. Behind them all is the basic choice of an affirmative view of history. Peace is a matter of hope.

> In our ordinary usage, people wage war,
>   . . . that is what they pay for
>   . . . that is what they risk their lives for.
> You make peace
>   . . . when war has become too costly,
>   . . . by ceasing to fight.

Peace is then a negation, an absence. That must be turned around. Peace is something to be waged

> . . . to plan for,
> . . . to train for,
> . . . to sacrifice for,
> . . . to die for.

Peace has institutional prerequisites that don't just happen; they need to be built.

Peace has attitudinal prerequisites that run against the grain of our nationalistic and racist cultures. They can be brought about only by experiences of unlearning, relearning.

We are given four glimpses of the alternative culture which the nations will create when they have come to Jerusalem.

The *first* is what we today call economic conversion. It is expressed in the phrase we know best from the prophecy: swords shall be transformed into plowshares.

The skills of smelting and smithing will be devoted no more to arming but to farming. The sharp edges will still be needed. In fact the edge of an agricultural implement needs to last longer and to cut more often than a weapon. So to make coulters instead of swords, and pruning knives instead of spears, will mean a technological advance, not a slowing down (just as today the armament industry is the least efficient and least competitive segment of the industrial economy). Thus the prophets' vision is not primitivism or "back to nature." It calls for the more expert and more productive use of the skills of smelter and smith.

The *second* change to be described is the renunciation of war as the institutional means of conflict resolution. It is not said that there will be no more nations—on the contrary. It is not said that they will have no differences, or no selfish interests. But because the Lord is their arbiter, they will make no plans for war.

Now we need to remember that war is an institution. It is not something that can happen without planning. A deed of violent *personal* self-defense may be spontaneous. A nonviolent action may sometimes be spontaneous (although the best ones are

usually planned). A deed of reconciliation may be a decision of
the moment (although even when such creative gestures seem to
be quite spontaneous, they are most often also the product of indirect premeditation and the expression of a gradually learned
lifestyle).

But a war cannot be spontaneous. It must be studied for. It is
complex and costly. It demands enormous organization to do
things that are not done every day. It needs skills different from
those of wholesome daily life. If you don't prepare for war, you
won't have war. The prophet says that they won't prepare,
thereby aligning himself with the many other places in the psalms
and the prophets where the end of war is announced as part of the
prophets' hope.

The vision is not (in these texts) that human nature will be
miraculously changed, so as to have no more conflict. It is rather
that human culture will be reprogrammed, by knowing the Law
and by the ministry of a new kind of Judge, who (as another song
in the second part of the book of Isaiah says it):

> will not rest
> until he has brought justice
>   to the ends of the earth.

Our text says:

> Torah will go out from Zion
>   and Yahweh's oracle from Jerusalem.
> He will arbitrate disputes between nations
>   and will act as a mediator for many nations.

It may well be that the original meaning of these terms
would have combined the kind of verdict that a judge issues on
the basis of evidence and the judicatory oracle which in other religions and also in ancient Israel was spoken by a priestly or prophetic voice in the temple. One scholar suggests that *torah* in verse
3b does not connote "law" in a general sense, the mosaic Law, or
general religious teaching. Rather, it refers to "instruction" in the
sense of a specific particular judgment as in Deuteronomy 17:11

where the word parallels *mishpat*, "judgment." That an oracle of judgment is intended is confirmed by the parallel, "word of Yahweh." A temple is then a priestly or prophetic supreme court for the nations. There is no distinction between teaching and adjudicating.

The *third* image is one of economic renewal. Everyone will have his own plot of productive land. Everyone will have a personal place for meaningful work: a vine and a fig tree.

To use modern terms, this is not capitalism, where the tools of a person's work belong to someone else. Nor is it a central economy run by the sword, or even by King Yahweh. It is not a market system so regulated that the most enterprising people come to own it all. It is economy of jubilee—a fresh start for everyone.

If we want to move beyond liking the poetry of the vision of Isaiah and Micah to living its promise, we might need to know which of these traits come first and which enables the other. Does the economic conversion enable the technological conversion? Or is it the other way around?

The *fourth* statement is the briefest: there will be no one more to fear.

Is the fear taken away and then they can relinquish their arms? Or does the arms reduction itself do away with the fear? Again we must ask which is cause and which is symptom.

In any case, the promise is not a disembodied, weightless heaven, nor a placeless eternity. It is a transformation of human existence within and not beyond its economic, cultural, and political nature.

The transformation is at the point of the reasons for *fear*.

One of the strange paradoxes of our national language game is the use of the word "security." "Internal security" means having people spying on our citizens. "National security" means military planning, especially developing equipment and strategies for retaliation.

To be authentically safe does not mean that to every threat one can pose a counterthreat. It means either that the threat is not there, or that one chooses not to fear it. The prophets, Jesus, and the early Christians faced real threats, but they chose not to fear them. Some of them faced martyrdom, but they did not fear it. It was given to them—by grace through faith—not to fear but to love.

Is learning the law still a good thing? We are the heirs of a strong mood of rejection of law. We have inherited from Martin Luther, coming down through the history of pietism and revival, a fear that learning or doing the law might get in the way of salvation. Most recently existentialism as a philosophy and the companion psychologies of self-fulfillment and authenticity have restated that pietist conviction in secular words. To that are added old echos of anti-Semitism (because we blame the Jews for the Law) and new resonances of intergenerational rebellion. So "legalism" has become a bad word and "freedom" is "in."

But is it really good to be above the Law? Or do we still need, as the prophets thought the nations needed it, to hear guidance from the Lord? We should remember that in the original Hebrew mood, "Torah" meant not so much "rules" but rather "guidance/instruction."

A second question we shall need to study is the choice, also put before us before our pietistic history, between spirituality and history. Religious renewal has often pointed away from the material world. Sometimes it called people from the city to the desert. It changed the agenda from matter to spirit, from the outwardly verifiable to the inward ineffable, from behaving to feeling, from doing to being. What should we then do with the very material form of this vision? Should we distill from it some inward spiritual meaning not dependent on its outward form? Or would it still guide us, although not literally, to be told that the prophets envision peace as having an economic shape, a technological shape, and a judicial shape?

Nothing about this text—and the many others like it—authorizes us to depreciate the text's real historical substance. Peace has an economic shape, a technological shape, a judicial shape. That's why we have peace studies in American universities. Of

course the inward motivational side matters. Of course you have
to care personally. Of course love for the enemy must be personal,
must be sincere. But the nations are already at that point when
they say, "Let us go to Jerusalem; let us hear Yahweh's instruction." Now what they need is to learn and to have the time and
the space and the know-how to reconvert their economies, to
restructure their democracies so that their living together in peace
will have a fitting structure and not only goodwill.

We turn back to the text for one more observation. What is it
that brings in the nations to learn the law? The Israelites do not
send out conquering armies, like Assyria or Rome, or like
Jerusalem today. They do not even send out diplomats and trade
missions and technical experts and cultural exchanges, like
Solomon. They don't send out missionaries or emplorers like
Marco Polo. The peoples come freely. They are attracted by the
restoration of the city, which they can see on their own. They are
attracted by the visible power of God at work renewing his
people. It is the restoration of Jerusalem which draws them in. It is
not because they come with their tribute that Jerusalem is restored.

The phrase "let us go up" is the technical term for pilgrimage to a holy place.

It is probably also significant that special reference is made
here to "the God of Jacob," and not to the other names for God
which were current in Canaan. Titles like "the most high" or "the
great king" had been used for the God of Jerusalem before it became the Israelite capital. Here the reference is specifically to the
Israelite people.

The exultation of Jerusalem is not to be distinguished from
the renewal of the Israelite community. The nations come not because Jerusalem is a well-known ancient holy city with a famous
God, but because something has been done to the believing community of Jacob.

For years most of us have been inclined to look away from
the believing community and to ask only about what to do with
the world. We want a recipe to impose on others by law. But the

prophet, like Jesus on his later hilltop (Matthew 5), looks the other way. He asks first about the believing community. Jesus speaks specifically to his disciples; they leave the crowds and come up the mountain to hear him. He asks them to be different, to be visibly different

> . . . like a light,
> . . . like a city on a hill.

Their differentness, he says, is to be in the way their righteousness fulfills the law and goes beyond the law

> . . . beyond not killing to not hating,
> . . . beyond limiting vengeance to renouncing vengeance,
> . . . beyond loving the neighbor to loving the enemy.

He does not ask first, "Can you run a government that way?" He asks first, "What is God like?" and calls his disciples to be like that. The God who loves his enemies is the original peace-maker.

Jesus invites his disciples first to be different. Then we can see how that faithfulness will make ripples around the world. He does not first ask how to tailor our ethics so as to enable us to get into offfice or to make the law. The nations may learn how to do that, but only if they see a restored Jerusalem whose citizens are different because they believe.

Now where does this promise leave us? Has it been fulfilled or is it still in the future? Are we to see ourselves from the Hebrew perspective as the Gentiles being drawn in? Are we to see ourselves from the messianic perspective as the Gentiles being drawn in? Are we to see ourselves from the messianic perspective as part of the city already restored? Or do we await it? Or are we in process of experiencing it? Are we the disciples who as Jesus retreats from the crowds gather around him on the hill to be told that the newness and fullness with which their deeds live out the law will lead others to glorify their heavenly Father?

If we do see ourselves, if we see all Christians in the claim that this new age has already begun, that Messiah has come, that the city on the hill has already been raised up, then we have to face a new challenge which is not stated in the text itself, but is the product of the intervening centuries.

It is important, if we want to understand why the Christian West has done so badly by the war question, to admit the major mistakes of the Christian past. It is too easy to confess the sins of the Constantines and the Charlemagnes, the Calvins and the Cromwells and the Kaisers. If repentance is to be part of a continuing confession, then we must admit that we have all failed to be the city on the hill.

Christianity is linked in Arab eyes with the Crusades; in Asian eyes with Empire. Since the fourth century Christian churches have justified war as much as they have restrained it. Since the Renaissance, Christian preachers have ratified nationalism as much as they have transcended it. The churches did not restrain our own nation's sins against the continent's original inhabitants or imported slaves, against the Mexicans in the age of Thoreau or against the Cubans and the Filipinos in the age of Bryan. It is from the North Atlantic world, where the churches have the most to say, that two world wars were unleashed. It is not that Christians as a whole have tried and failed to build a peaceable city. It is that until recently they have thought it would be wrong to try, or (what amounts to the same thing) that the only way to do it was to win their wars.

Christian repentance is, however, not self-condemnation. It is a response to a gracious God, who, without our having merited it, gives us reason to hope.

Our time is one in which committed people feel impotent. This first prophetic image gives hope. The promise is God's work. It is not we who achieve his goal of restoring the city or his goals of bringing in the nations. The miracle is geological according to Isaiah, Micah, and Zechariah, or aeronautical according to Revelation. The Israelites have a part in that victory. They are to carry the report. They are to fit into the new order. They are to receive a new spirit and to give thanks. But they do not do it. God does it. God does it also through others—through pagan peoples who do not confess God's name, and through rulers who are seeking their own selfish benefit.

We need that answer to despair. But we may also need warnings against a too-easy hope. Our culture, more than any other in Christian history, sets us up for disappointment. This is not because we cannot do much. Rather, we can do more than most people have ever been able to do. Since the fourth century, church leaders in the Western world have had easy access to their rulers. Since the Magna Charta (very gradually), reforms and revolutions have brought to most people in our part of the world a sense that they share in ruling themselves. The last two centuries have brought new material and scientific resources to bear on our coming to think that we can do anything we want to do. In our century explicit charters assure the limits of government and the voice even of minorities.

It may be precisely because our own world and its Anglo-Saxon political heritage makes the most promises, and can record the best past achievements on the path toward institutionalized respect for all subjects, that we have become the least realistic and the most easily disappointed. We are short of wind for the long struggle, because there are muscles we have not used.

To this the biblical witness speaks only indirectly. We cannot find in the Bible the failure of the West. Yet we do find the failure of national kingship in the history of Israel. We do find a prophetic critique of the ordinary power structures of the ancient near eastern world, and the progressive dismantling of the vision of human dignity which kingship had carried. That had already begun to happen when Isaiah and Micah spoke. It was already further along by the time this common text had found its way into the final versions of their written prophecies.

But all of us continue to be trained by the relatively privileged history of the Christian West. We are predisposed to link truth and success, in ways that stand on the shoulders of the time of the establishment of religion in the so-called Christian world. That means that we are out of phase with the power realities of the modern world, even of our own world, which does not remember establishment nearly as well as we do, to say nothing of the premodern world which is still with us in Iran and Afghanistan and central Africa, or the quite non-Western cultures that still live in India or Japan.

So I leave you with the question genuinely unfinished. The more seriously we take God's promise that his peacemaking will is for this world, the more consistently we claim (by calling Jesus the Christ) that the messianic age has begun, the more urgent becomes our search today for a common sense of how the renewal of God's people will call the nations into God's program.

Given at New Call to Peacemaking, Elizabethtown, Pennsylvania, June 18, 1982; at Briar Cliff College, Sioux City, Iowa, April 18, 1983; and at Whitworth College, Spokane, Washington, February 24, 1984.

9

The Broken Wall

I have been entrusted by God
with the grace he meant for you.
It was by a revelation
that I was given the knowledge of the mystery. . . .
If you read my words
you will have some idea of the depths
that I see in the mystery of Christ. . . .
This mystery that has now been revealed through the Spirit
. . . was not known to anyone in past generations. . . .
I, who am less than the least of all the saints,
have been entrusted with this special grace,
Not only of proclaiming to the pagans
the infinite treasure of Christ,
But also of explaining
how the mystery is to be dispensed.
Ephesians 3:2-9, JB

There are other writings (especially Galatians) where the biographical dimension of what Paul is talking about here is spelled out more fully. There are others (especially 2 Corinthians) which go at greater depth into the sensitive matters of personal self-esteem and authority and how Paul's ministry as proclaimer is spelled out in his leadership style. But this text may be the one in which Paul makes most strongly his claim to a unique place in the history of revelation for his own ideas and ministry.

If this were a technical study we would have to look at some introductory questions with care. Who were the believers at Ephesus? What was going on there that led Paul to write them this letter at this time? Did the apostle write this text with his own hand, or did he authorize a secretary to write it on his behalf? Or was it finally put on papyrus by one of his disciples, using his ideas and confident of being able to write in his spirit? For our purposes there is no need to resolve those questions. If it should be the case that the letter was written a little later by Paul's disciples, then the strong statement it makes about the centrality of his ministry would be even more striking.

Four times in our text Paul used the word "mystery." A mystery is information that is hidden. It may be a fact which we are trying to find out. That meaning has given its tone to the name of a certain kind of paperback novel. It may mean religious information reserved for especially initiated devotees, but that is not what is meant here. Here what it means is rather like a military battle plan which was previously hidden from the public eye, although it was present in the mind of the strategist, but is now visible for all to see because the acting out of what was planned is itself its revelation.

The same phenomenon is evident if we look at the wars of recent times: at the British reconquest of the Malvinas, the Israeli conquest of Lebanon, the American occupation of Grenada. Six weeks before the attack no one could guess how it would go. After the campaign, the strategy is manifest.

Through all the ages that purpose had been kept hidden in God, the Creator of everything. What was that divine purpose? As Paul says in 3:3, he had just described it briefly in chapter 2, so we reach back for that description.

> You who used to be apart from us
>   have been brought very close
>   by the blood of Christ. (2:3)

"You" means the Gentiles. When he says

> You were excluded from membership of Israel;
> aliens with no part in the
>   covenants with their promise . . .
> without hope and without God . . . .

Paul is not speaking primarily of the personal rebellion and lostness or fallenness of each individual unbeliever. He is describing the status of the Gentile world as "world," as a whole. The covenant is a relationship. The Gentiles are out of it, until something happens to call them into it, and that is what has just happened. The covenant is information. The Gentiles don't know about it until it is manifested.

So there are two kinds of people: those with and those without a share in holy history. This is not a matter of moral advantage. Those with the knowledge may be worse off because they are more accountable. They may be bad persons. But they have been entrusted with a privilege. They know the name and the will of the Creator and sovereign of history.

This is not a peculiarity of religion or of this religion. Any information creates that kind of division. Especially does any information that becomes known through particular events necessarily create such a division. Some insiders know which way the stock market will go. Some people can use computers and some cannot. Some people are in on any story and some others are not. But if the privileged information which some have and others do not is not just some narrative facts, or some philosophical password, but the revelation of the purposes of God, what Paul calls the "covenant of promise," then what they are outside of is salvation.

So there are two kinds of people: Those with and those without a religious world vision. Those with and those without a defined moral culture. Those with and those without a share in the sacred story. Those with and those without a religious education.

As I already said, the people with are not necessarily better people. Many Jews and many Christians have been bad people. Many outsiders have been good people. People "with" are not better off. They may be worse off because they are more accountable for their greater power.

That division is deeper than the divisions of nation, class, and race, although it sometimes correlates with those divisions, and then that makes the peacemaking problem worse. That alienation is the problem, which Paul says, the work of Christ resolves.

> He is the peace between us.
> He has made the two into one.
> He has broken down the barrier
>   which used to keep them apart.
> He destroyed in his person the hostility
>   caused by the rules of the Law.
> This was to create one single new humanity
>   in himself out of the two of them.
>
> Later he came to bring the good news of peace;
> Peace to you who were far away (you Gentiles);
> Peace to those who were near at hand (us Jews).
> Through him both of us have
>   in the one Spirit
>   our way to come to the Father;
>   So you Gentiles
>   are no longer aliens
>   or visitors;
>   you are citizens like all the saints.

The death of Christ is spoken of in the New Testament in many different ways. Sometimes it is spoken of as a sacrifice, sometimes as a ransom. This time it breaks down a wall. There was of course literally a wall of masonry in Jerusalem, separating the outer court where the Gentiles could come from the temple court proper. Is Paul referring to that wall itself as a symbol? Or is his meaning still more indirectly symbolic?

What Jesus did was to remove the barrier between the "in" people and the "out" people. Our ordinary picture is of the cross as reconciling me to God over the barrier of my sins, and reconciling you to God over the barrier of your sins, and reconciling her to God over the barrier of her sins so that as a result we find ourselves all (one by one) together in this new saved status. In this text the logic runs the other way. The barrier is not anybody's sin. The barrier is the historical fact of separate stories. It is the fact that "we Jews have the law and you Gentiles don't." It is not a barrier of guilt, but of culture and of communication. It is not a barrier between each person and God but between one group and another.

The causal line does not run where it does in many modern religious (and for that matter secular) views of the human predicament. It is not the case that inner or personal peace comes first, with the hope that once the inward condition is set right then the restored person will do some social good. In this text it is the other way around. Two estranged *histories* are made into one. Two hostile *communities* are reconciled. Two conflicting *lifestyles* flow together.

Lest we should think that the distance between Jew and Gentile is a matter of different theories or world views, the rest of the story makes clear how concrete the conflicts of style were and what they were about. We see more of that in the narrative of Acts, and still more in the practical guidance of Romans and 1 Corinthians, as well as in the debate with Peter which was recorded in Galatians. For theological reasons the Jews could not eat with Gentiles. Especially they could not if the meat being eaten had not been slaughtered in the Jewish way. Yet the basic religious celebration of the Christians (the messianic Jews) was a meal, a love feast. So Acts tells us twice about the viable compromise which they reached concerning the conditions for eating together. Three chapters of 1 Corinthians spell out Paul's own commitment to respecting that agreement. So concrete was the conflict, so formal and outward was the living-out of the peace which Jesus had made.

Before going one more step with the text, let us note some open questions.

(1) How did Paul get this way? What made him the privileged bearer of a new message abut the mystery of God's purposes? Did he first get a new idea from some sort of divine inspira-

tion and then go to act it out? Or was he first drawn into the movement of the spreading messianic faith in a way something like what the book of Acts recounts, and then had to think out under fire why that activity was proper?

(2) How did the cross break the wall? What happened was that Gentiles put to death a faithful Jew. How does that break the wall? Some people in the Jewish establishment had turned over to some people in the Gentile establishment the person who had opened the law to Gentiles. But how was it the law that killed him? How was his death the result of the rules of the law? That Paul says this is clear. How it makes sense is a question on which one would need more light from other texts. That is the task of what we call a "doctrine of the atonement." Jesus himself never described his death in just this way. Does that matter? But then the writings of Paul are earlier than the Gospels, where we read the words of Jesus. So if what Ephesians says were not true, if what Paul here describes happening had not really been working, we might not even have the Gospels.

There is one more step for us to take with our text. What does that peacemaking have to do with our peacemaking? As cosmic as Paul's language is, we still might believe that all that is going on is a one-time breaking of the Jew/Gentile barrier, and that that is a minor provincial event within the spread of Jewish religion. Now a few non-Jews can learn about monotheism and morality.

Paul claims much more that that. He asks the rhetorical question, Why was all this hidden through all the ages?

> So that it should be only now
> that the sovereignties and powers (JB),
> that the rulers and authorities (NEB and NIV; other versions say
> "principalities and powers"),
> that the cosmic rulers (JHY),
> should learn through the church
> what God's comprehensive wisdom really is,
> exactly according to the plan
> which he had from all eternity
> in Christ Jesus our Lord.
>
> *Ephesians 3:10-11*

Now what these "cosmic authorities" were in Paul's mind is not easy to say in modern terms. They are not human persons. Yet they influence human events and structures. What we call the state, the economy, the media, ideology—these are their instruments. (The most accessible exposition of the thought of Paul in modern terms is the book *Christ and the Powers* by Hendrik Berkhof. Berkhof draws from Paul's writings nine texts where there are such references.)

The Hebrew prophets had said that it was the restoration of the holy city that would call the nations in. Now it is the creation of a new kind of community which communicates to the cosmic powers.

Paul makes it clear that this wider cosmic realm is impacted by the cross and the ascension of Jesus Christ. Frequently, in passing, Paul refers to these "powers" as if we knew what he meant. He certainly knew what he meant, and his readers must have known too.

Somehow the subservience of the fallen world to the fallen powers stands in correlation with the wall between Jew and Gentile. The structures which enslave us have a stake in keeping us apart. Nationalism, racism, mammonism, enslave us by dividing us, and they divide us by enslaving us. We could meditate a long time on that viciously circular truth.

These cosmic powers did not know that the goal of God from all eternity was to make one new humanity. They thought that the meaning of history was the prosperity of the free world, or the growth of the gross national product, or the spread of democracy across the globe (or of Nazism, or of Marxism, or whatever). Their vision of the meaning of history was divided and centered on domination. Paul helps us understand that their idolatry will be smashed and their pride will be sobered. The cosmic powers will not be destroyed, but they will be tamed, as they too will find their place in the new humanity.

They did not know (I was saying) that the goal of God from all eternity was to make one new humanity. Why did they not know it? Because it was only from the church that they should learn it. Only when it is a fact that Jewry and paganism are set at one (are "atoned"), only when Jew and Gentile are eating at the same table and lovingly adjusting their lifestyles this may happen without offense, only then can it be said to the powers that peace is God's purpose. So our job is cut out for us in our ongoing study of the text. How does our life reenact the melding of two histories and two cultures? Where does our banqueting celebrate the new humanity created by the crosses of our time breaking down the walls of our time so that the cosmic powers of our time can see what God is about?

If we are about what God is about, there will be crosses in our time to break down the walls of our time. If we are about what God is about, then our tribulations are glory. Let us close as Paul did:

> This is why we are bold enough
> to approach God in complete confidence
> through our faith in him . . . .
> Never lose confidence
> just because of the trials
> that I go through on your account:
> they are your glory.
>
> *Ephesians 3:12, JB*

Given at New Call to Peacemaking, Elizabethtown, Pennsylvania, June 19, 1982.

10

The Gift of Reconciliation

According to the Bible, the purpose of God always has a social shape. The purpose of God is peace in real human shared experience. In this text, Jesus instructs us most concretely how to go about that. He prescribes a procedure of conflict resolution.

> If your brother sins,
>   go reprove him,
>   between him and you alone.
> If he listens,
>   you have won your brother.
> If he does not listen,
>   take one or two others with you.
> The evidence of two or three witnesses
>   is required to sustain any charge . . . .
> Truly, what you bind on earth
>   shall be bound in heaven.
> What you loose on earth
>   shall be loosed in heaven.
>
> *Matthew 18:15-18*

Conflict resolution has in our time become a recognizable term. It is a social science, it is a subdiscipline of psychology, and it is a social service skill. I take note of that new development, not as support for the teachings of Jesus, but as a currently understood name for what Jesus here offers.

This teaching may very well be so commonsensical and so functional, and even so familiar from your church tradition, that you would be asking why it should be worth the trouble to talk about it directly. Yet for others it may be new, unfamiliar, or even in principle, questionable. It does run counter to some patterns of good manners in our polite society, where a large part of social maturity consists in learning to keep our hands off other people's business.

I was speaking recently with a psychologist who is a member of a Christian commune. He reported that people who look from outside at communal life think that it must be very hard to give up control over one's money. As a matter of fact, he testified, that is not the case. On the other hand, people would think from the outside that it would be a simple matter to live up to the idea of regular fraternal admonition, being open about offenses. But that is always difficult, he said, even after years of experience in the communal movement.

Because this text is so simple and its command is so evident, what I can say about it cannot be as far-reaching as the comments on the other passages. I must begin more with the nuts and bolts of what the words mean.

An important, though apparently small issue, is two words (only five letters in the Greek) which the older translations retain and some of the newer translations rightly omit. The older translations say, "If your brother sins *against you* . . . ." This is an understandable but misleading change. It gives the impression that the reason to go to my brother is my need and not that of the offender—that what needs to be done is discharging my anger, not that the guilty party needs to be corrected and forgiven.

This change may give the impression that if I am not the victim of the offense I should keep my hands off. It may give the impression that if I am thick-skinned, or if I have a high tolerance level, so that I don't really mind, or if I am a bighearted person, magnanimous, I won't make an issue of the offense. In all of these ways those five letters lead us astray. They are not in the best text of the Greek nor in the best new English translations. They are not in the parallel passages of Luke 17 and Leviticus 19. That was a small question to begin with, yet a weighty one. Now we move to the wider frame.

Chapter 18 of Matthew's Gospel is all about forgiveness. Before our passage there was the warning against offending a little one. There was a call to make sacrifices, giving up even an eye or a hand, rather than to offend. Then there was the parable of the lost sheep. After our passage there is Peter's question, "How often must I forgive?" Then there is the unforgiving debtor, concluding with, "God will not forgive you, unless you forgive your brother."

So the purpose of the approach to the brother or sister is to forgive. The reason to forgive my brother or sister is that God has forgiven me. That is why it does not matter whether the offense was against me. It does not matter whether the damage was great or small.

For some, the purpose of what they call "church discipline" is to preserve the reputation of the church. For others it is to "teach" the community's standards, and show young people the seriousness of sin. For still others it is punishment.

Not for Jesus. For him the only point is pardon. If he listens, you have won back your brother. That's all. No prerequisites, no follow-up.

There is something unique about this one Christian duty, which is not said with the same simplicity about any other duty, precisely because it is more than just a moral duty. Most of the time, New Testament statements about what God requires of us are that we should believe and obey, but seldom is our obedience a condition. Here we are told far more precisely that our forgiving is a part of our being forgiven. That is also said in the rest of Matthew 18, and in the Lord's Prayer, in Jesus' comment on the Lord's Prayer, and twice by Paul.

There may be some people who can "forgive themselves," in the sense of the simple mental operation whereby they tell themselves, "I am forgiven" or even "I am okay." Or they may tell themselves, "No one should be offended at what I did" or "I am not to blame." But if they can, the meaning of pardon is cheapened. Most people, if they told themselves they were forgiven, would not believe themselves, and rightly not.

There may be others who can forgive another person without telling them (they are able to cease to reckon the offense against the other person), but that too is a cheapening of the relationship, because it withholds good news.

Our discussion of the hilltop city (chapter 8) brought up the question, "How shall we relate the gospel that came to Jerusalem to all the other people?" We asked what will bring the nations in. The consideration of the broken wall (chapter 9) made us ask how it relates to other people if the Gentiles are able to become part of the one new humanity without becoming Jews. Can people make peace without being Christian? Some of us would say, "Of course." Others would ask, "How could that be?" Does that not bypass the centrality (for the person needing to be saved) of the issue of faith, or the centrality (for the believer) of the duty to evangelize? All of these texts tell us that there is a two-way link between our peacemaking and divine forgiveness.

One unspoken command in Jesus' instruction is almost as important as the explicit one. When Jesus says, "Go to him alone" that means, "Don't go to others." Don't spread the bad news. Don't activate the gossip network. Don't line up allies on your side of the issue before confronting the sister or brother. Don't amplify your view of the thing. Don't isolate the offender, increase the distance, and reinforce your anger, if your intent is really to pass on the forgiveness which you have received and keep receiving from God.

The effort to reconcile widens with more than one attempt. The reference to "two or three witnesses" is not something Jesus made up. It is part of the process prescribed by the Old Testament law. In the awareness that any denunciation might be not all of the truth, the "two or three witnesses" whom Moses called for are as much a check on my testimony as they are a reinforcement of my pressure on the offender. They mediate rather than reinforcing, and if I want to forgive, I will want them to mediate. Their entry into the conversation gives both of us a chance to reassess and maybe to back off.

But all the efforts may fail. The three successive widening phases of pleading (which would normally mean more than three meetings) may conclude that we have on this matter no common value or commitment—that forgiveness is not wanted. Then we face a prospect which the early Christian church and the synagogue probably had less trouble with than we do: "Treat him like an outsider." Admit the fact that he has excluded himself—that he does not care to be reconciled.

In our age of pluralism, when we are less sure of our own standards, in our age of individualism in which we say that everyone must follow her own conscience, we are embarrassed about being this serious. This phrase of Jesus is misunderstood unless we remember how Jesus treated the tax collectors. He didn't hold it especially against them that their involvement with the Romans was bad. He related to them personally. He went into their homes. He compared some of them favorably with the Pharisees, and yet he did call them to repent.

We are afraid in our modern polite pluralism to tell anyone that our communion with them has limits. Thus we jeopardize the possiblity of deepening solidarity in our own ranks, and we sacrifice the possibility of moving the offender to genuine reconciliation, by not daring to say, "You have left us. You have denied your fellowship with us. We want you to be one of us, but we can't have you as one of us as long as you persist. . . .

That weakness on our part has some good explanations. They are not in the text but they are in our own history. Some past abuses have destroyed the credibility of the church's efforts to forgive. Those abuses still resonate when we use the term "church discipline." In some of our traditions the verb was "to church" and in others "to deacon." Such phrases referred to a process looking a little like what Jesus said, but subtly different, applied for other reasons. Standards have been applied of whose correctness the offender was not convinced, or to which the offender had never freely adhered. Standards have been applied by clerical authorities instead of by the persons nearest the offense. They have been applied for the wrong reasons: to punish, to defend authority, to prevent change. They have been applied unfairly, dealing more harshly with the sins of the weak than with those of the strong. You may extend the list of abuses, there are more.

But we should not have let the abuses frighten us away from the proper gospel process. It is not our own concern that we fail to discharge, but the Lord's. He is the one who wants the forgiving to go on.

> What you bind on earth
> is bound in heaven.

To "bind" or to "loose" comes from the vocabulary of the rabbis. "Binding" action is action which will hold firm. The act of forgiving on God's behalf is so powerful that it is described like a power of attorney, or like an ambassador's credentials. The parallel in John 20 says, "Those whose sins you forgive, are forgiven." How can *we* do that? The answer is that we can't. God does it through us.

The next verses, "Where two or three agree in my name, I am there with them," are not talking about the general value of small groups or of common prayer. The "two or three" are the witnesses of verse 16. The agreement among them (the Greek term is the same as our word "symphony") is their common reading of the case. The presence of Christ is what empowers their conversation and validates their conclusion. What they decide stands in heaven because he was there with them deciding it.

In John 20 we read:

> He breathed on them and said,
> "Receive the holy breath.
> Those whose sins you forgive, are forgiven."

So much for the words of the text. We have laid upon us a

procedure for concrete peacemaking, a pattern for practice and training in the acting out of the making of peace.

In conclusion I can only name the directions in which further elaboration would be fruitful.

(1) To bind and to loose, in the language of the rabbis, meant not only to forgive but also the process of moral discernment. There is an intimate link between forgiving and making ethical decisions.

(2) This is a strategically important passage in the total New Testament. It is the only place we find the word "church" reported as being used by Jesus himself. Its weight is accented by the account of Paul's asking the Christians in Corinth to use this procedure instead of going to the Gentile courts (1 Corinthians 6:1-8), and by the explicit command closing the letter of James (5:19-20).

(3) This concern had a central place in the Reformation of the 16th century. There it was described with the label "rule of Christ," a term used by Martin Luther and Martin Bucer, as well as by the Anabaptists. The Anabaptists understood that this procedure is the nonviolent Christian alternative to the sword. It is the instrument of Reformation, the way to go about purifying the church. It became one of the three "ordinances" for which the Anabaptists believed that they had a command of the Lord.

(4) There is growing awareness today of the strategic importance of this kind of binding and reconciling conversation in the maintenance of community and the resolution of social problems. As I said, conflict resolution has become a social science. Mediation and arbitration have become professional social skills. The world knows, even though the church hesitates to recognize it, that this pattern of peacemaking is both possible and indispensible.

Given at New Call to Peacemaking, Elizabethtown, Pennsylvania, June 20, 1982.

11

Your Hope Is Too Small

This is the only one of the Servant Songs to be auto-biographical and personal. Isaiah 42 refers to the Servant in the third person, with God speaking:

Behold my Servant
  Whom I uphold
My chosen
  in whom my soul delights

Chapter 53 is also in the third person, but here it is the onlooker who is speaking:

Who has believed what we have heard?
To whom has the Lord's arm been revealed?
He grew up before him
  like a young plant,
  like a root out of dry ground.

In chapter 50 the Servant speaks in the first person, with the text most like what we have here, but one does not see behind it any specific event or any specific drama:

The Lord God has given me
  The disciple's tongue

> That I may know how to sustain with a word
>   the weary;
> Morning by morning he wakens my ear
>   to listen like a disciple.

Here alone in chapter 49, the Servant speaks about himself, his growth, his thoughts, his despair, and his hope. He speaks as well to the world. This is the only song which is not addressed to the Israelites. In this respect it constitutes a missionary high point of the Hebrew Bible.

It is simplest to think of the Servant as a particular person— perhaps a younger member of the royal family in exile who saw himself, or whom the prophets saw as being prepared for a very special usefulness.

> Yahweh called me before I was born,
> From my mother's womb he pronounced my name.
> He made my mouth a sharp sword,
> and hid me in the shadow of his hand.
> He made me into a sharpened arrow,
> and concealed me in his quiver.
> He said to me, "You are my servant
> in whom I shall be glorified."

This man trusted the promise of the prophet that Israel would be restored. In line with that hope he trusted that he would be needed. Like the paperboy in the Horatio Alger novel, like Abraham Lincoln and Richard Nixon, he waited in the wings until his time would come. But it didn't; it never did.

He was never drawn from the shadow of the quiver to be pulled against the bowstring. A polished arrow that stays hidden in the quiver is no arrow at all. Israel was not restored, and they didn't need him to lead the parade.

It is simplest to speak thus of the servant as an individual; but for our purposes it would be no different if, as some scholars believe, the meaning was centered upon a small group or the whole people of Israel.

The normal response to defeat is resignation. Verse 4 does not speak childlike trust but unwillingness to face failure by name:

> All the while my cause was with Yahweh,
> My reward with my gods.
> I was honored in the eyes to Yahweh;
> my God was my strength.

The claim is that despite failure one is in the right. I trust that God supports me even if events do not. To give up on a cause while claiming a moral victory as if the failure were itself a proof of one's integrity is a posture which avoids recognizing the failure as such.

This brings us to the center of the prophecy. The servant had been called to restore Israel and he had failed. Now God speaks again:

> Now Yahweh has spoken,
> He who formed me in the womb to be his servant,
> to bring Jacob back to him,
> and to gather Israel to him.

And what will Yahweh say? Will he say, "If at first you don't succeed, try again"? Will he say, "The third time is the charm"? Will he say, "We know what we did wrong. We have the bugs out of it now"?

Yahweh does not say that at all:

> It is not enough for you to be my servant
> to restore the tribes of Jacob
> and bring back the survivors of Israel.

This is a new prophetic word. What you failed to do before is too small a task. You thought your whole calling was to restore the tribes of Jacob and lead back the descendants of Israel (the older translations here say, the preserved, the leftovers, the debris.) What you felt had at least been an honorable try, entitling you to the vicarious vindication which God gives like a purple heart to those who fail in worthy causes—that is too small a task, too slight a hope.

> I will make you the light of the nations so that my salvation may reach to the ends of the earth.

What you failed to do is too small a task. I am going to save the world. And now the servant himself comes in the midst of his defeat, while still defeated, standing there beaten, and proclaims this very promise to the nations themselves—to the very kings and princes who (according to verse 7) despise and abhor him.

It lies at the heart of the great Puritan heritage that has made America the nation that it is and has made our churches what they are that we identify God's success as our very own. Indeed one of the most frequent and most concrete meanings of the phrase, "God has blessed" in American pious usage is to describe the success of a church agency in increasing its income. This had been the assumption the servant was making—that God's visible success would correlate with his own prosperous future. Was not "servant of God" the term used to honor a triumphant king in the ancient Near East?

But God says, "No. What I can use is your failure. We will never succeed in restoring Israel; that would be too slight a vision. We shall reach the nations.

"Ezra and Nehemiah will not restore Israel. The Maccabees will not restore Israel. The Zealots will not restore Israel. But in that failure, in that rejection and suffering, my righteousness will be carried to the end of the earth."

We live in a time and in a culture in which Christians are divided by competing visions of what it would mean for the people of God to be "restored." The word "restore" is a backward-looking verb. It assumes "the good old days" when times were not so far out of joint, when the church and her world were more in step. To get back to them there are two ways to proceed.

Those whose posture is defensive, whose adolescent identity crisis was their capitulation to the community, whose "growing up" amounted to their acceptance of norms of their parents— persons joining the church of their fathers, under these circumstances will mean by "restore" precisely that. They will see the flaws in what is new. To them the task of the church is to reinforce the ancient landmarks and to pick up the pieces of who we once were.

But there are those others whose stance is more critical. There are those whose adolescent identity and experience was that (in the age of Dr. Spock and Aquarius) their parents capitulated to them. They prefer renewal to restoration. They see the flaws in what was and they want something new.

But both parties have the same deep hope for their people, once restored according to their respective recipes, to have something of the past prominence of Puritan churches.

Now if this were our theme we could take some more time to ask whether the good old days ever were that. We could probe whether the two contradictory visions of renewal are as contradictory or as clear as they seem. But for now we must return to the hope of the servant:

> I rose to honor in the Lord's sight;
> I was going to be in on the victory.

Our culture cannot distinguish efficacy from truth. William James and John Dewey told us, didn't they, translating into secular terms the old Puritan vision, that the truth is what works? So of course we learned to ask if the effect we hoped for will be achieved by the action we propose. If people ought to be evangelized we set up a board of evangelism. If the Christian church needs leaders we produce them in a special seminary program (even though much past leadership was prepared in other ways). If Israel is to be restored, the servant must lead the caravan. We cannot conceive of a value system that would say the truth is what gets crucified. Even our nonresistance needs some kind of proof that it is likely to "work."

Now if we had the time we could argue at some length that such a view is logically weak because such "pragmatic" analysis assumes a closed causal system where no one else—not even God—is a free agent. But the point of our passage is not critical logic. It is a word of the Lord spoken to the servant in his defeat.

"You do not sight down the line of your success to my victory." It is because we want to do that that we are predisposed to be unable to grasp the meaning of the cross. We filter the cross through a doctrine of the atonement to make of it a way to restore our good standing before God, instead of being overwhelmed at how mightily the Servant shares our bad standing.

We make of the cross a sign of power. The crusade is a war for the sake of the cross. A bishop wears a cross on his breast to show he can do things other people can't. We use "crusade" to designate a mass evangelistic effort or any other good cause where we focus all of the skills and the power we can muster so that our triumph will be sure because we are on God's side.

> Conquer we must
> for our cause, it is just
> and this is our motto
> in God is our trust.

Since we are not able to deal with defeat as a pattern of God's victory, neither can we be as honest as the Servant finally was with the fact that we are defeated. We can always find ways to read signs of the times more hopefully, like the Washington executives who were always seeing light at the end of the tunnel in Vietnam. We busy ourselves with picking up the pieces, like the Barthian Protestantism which restored the integrity of the Reformation message—but with no audience in the churches. Like the resurgence of religion in suburbia, we restore the church as the bastion of family values—"Families that pray together stay together" or "You can lift your life"—but with no moral cutting edge.

Might it be, sometime, that our world will be sick enough of its power that it might become clear that only a savior who could fail—only a shamed, rejected, crucified Messiah—has anything to say? As long as hope for the resurrection for the preserved of Israel is our hope, we can find plenty to do, puttering around in our archives and soliciting endowment for our spiritual retirement communities, and not notice that salvation history has taken another road. If we were perceptive, we would see that this isn't working.

How much better if we heard the new word that the prophet has spoken, if we could be as honest as the Servant.

I have labored in vain;
I have spent my strength for nothing.

The message is no less true today and no less needed, even
though the restorative shapes we give it are dependent on our
past. The world's need for, and openness to, a vital proclamation
of the word and the cross is as great as ever. Yet the Protestant
faith in its mainstream forms, with its institutional vehicles, its
boards and councils, as a moving of God's Spirit for the saving of
the world, providing insight and discipline against the idolatry of
the age, is no longer its vehicle.

The need of the world for, and its openness to, the news of
the victory over death of Jesus the servant Messiah and the call to
new life to which he resurrects those who forsake all to follow him
in discipleship is greater than ever before. So while we discuss
whether "nonviolence" or "nonresistance" is the right word for
describing our reasons for not killing, a Southern Christian
Leadership Council had to rise up in the 1960s to tell us the meaning of the cross for race relations. While we pacifists discussed
whether it is our place to tell the government how to do its business, campuses had to rise in the 1970s to tell us how wrong was
the war in Vietnam. Roman Catholic bishops have to rise up in
the 1980s to tell us to stop nuclear war.

Might it be, at least partially, the case that our confidence in
our adequacy for the task of "restoring," our hope—too small
hope—in our own mission is what makes us ineligible for the
overarching resurrection promised by the all-sufficient grace
whose strength is made perfect in weakness?

What the Servant needs to do in order that kings and princes
who despise and abhor him may be convicted by the evidence of
his election is not to work just a little harder or just a little more
humbly at the old job he had failed at before, not to defend his
last thread of self-esteem by claiming at least a moral victory, and
not to wait just a little more patiently in the shadow under the
cover of the hand of the Lord. What the Servant had to do was to
admit and accept his own defeat, and to accept in faith the salvation of the Lord.

The test of the Servant's readiness to be a participant in God's victory is his acceptance of his own brokenness.

Yet this is not to search for brokenness for its own sake, after the style of certain kinds of pietism or certain kinds of psychotherapy. There is no morbid joy in how bad I feel, no theological glorification of tribulation or *Anfechtung*. There is no pride in how tragically I take suffering. The defeat of the Servant is defeat in his devotion to the cause to which God had called him. The promised resurrection is a triumph not for the vindicated Servant but for the Holy One who has chosen him. We are not to glory in our strength. Neither are we to glory in our weakness but in that treasure which is seen in earthen vessels.

It is too slight a task for you, my servants, to regroup and reassure the children of church people, to keep communities alive through the last stages of acculturation. It is too slight a task to provide an accepting milieu and a listening ear to the angry children of suburbia.

I want to make you a light to the nations. In that missionary miracle whereby God makes the nations see his light and come to Jerusalem to learn the law, the servant will be used after all.

In the miracle which might follow if Christians in our day were found in the stance of the Servant, we might also find ourselves, unexpectedly, by grace alone through faith, usable.

Perhaps (though not necessarily) even our church organizations and agencies, our councils of churches and our ministerial self-understandings can be reborn. That is not for us to decide or even to ask. What tools God will use is none of our business. Remember our Lord's last words in our last Gospel:

> If it be my will
> That it should be your brother who survives
> Until I come, what is that to you?
> As for you, follow me.

Originally presented on May 29, 1970 at Associated Mennonite Biblical Seminaries, Elkhart, Indiana.

12

Turn, Turn

Once upon a time, there was a religious and ethnic minority group threatened by the economic and political superiority of the surrounding culture. Living under the sway of a nation whose economic and military power dominated the world, this little people was seriously demoralized. Through its institutions of education and entertainment, the dominant cultural power of the ruler's religion was beginning to brainwash the younger generation of the minority group, estranging them from the language and the lifestyle which their elders had brought with them when they had come to the country, and had kept intact for centuries.

This tension between the wider cosmopolitan world and the inner enclave of inherited faith was reinforced by another polarity: the tension between young and old. The young, with their normal inclination to call into question what they are told is self-evident, found further leverage for their doubt in the fact that the wider society held little esteem for the faith of their fathers, conceding to it the respect one grants any toughly held conviction but hardly impressed by its claim for truth.

Their elders, on the other hand, committed as the elders usually are to the defense of what has been always believed, were only confirmed in their conviction that the whole wide world of cosmopolitan culture was an evil thing as they observed the temptations, the doubts, and the estrangement to which their daughters and sons were giving in. It seemed to follow logically, did it not, that the defense of the inherited faith would be worth the price, if necessary, even of cultural isolation and economic deprivation if it were possible to save the heritage by retreating and retrenching? In the tension between accommodation by the young and the elders' separatist defensiveness, the concerned and insightful observer had reason to doubt whether the faith of this heroic minority would survive for much longer. The danger was real that the link between the generations would snap, and that whatever would survive, if anything did, would not be the same religion.

The once-upon-a-time I am talking about was in the fifth century before Christ, just before the age of Nehemiah. Under the rule of Persia, having lost all prospect of the restoration of the kind of independent political development on which their self-respect had been dependent, the Jewish nation faced what today would be called a crisis of identity. It was to this situation that the prophet spoke whose book we call Malachi. The closing words of this book stick in our minds more than most of the prophets' messages, partly because of the hazard of their placement at the very end of the Old Testament, partly because of the place of Elijah in the expectation of Jesus' contemporaries, and perhaps partly because of their use in Handel's *Messiah.*"

> Behold, I send my messenger
> to prepare the way before me,
> and the Lord whom you seek
> will suddenly come to his temple;
>
> the messenger of the covenant
> in whom you delight,
> behold, he is coming,
> says the Lord of hosts.
>
> But who can endure the day of his coming,
> and who can stand when he appears?

For he is like a refiner's fire
and like fullers' soap;

he will sit as a refiner
and purifier of silver,
and he will purify the sons of Levi
and refine them like gold and silver,
till they present right offerings to the Lord.

Then the offering of Judah and Jerusalem
will be pleasing to the Lord
as in the days of old
and as in former years. . . .

For behold, the day comes,
burning like an oven,
when all the arrogant and all the evildoers will be stubble;
the day that comes
shall burn them up,
says the Lord of hosts,
so that it will leave them
neither root nor branch.

But for you who fear my name,
the Son of Righteousness shall rise,
with healing in his wings. . . .

Behold, I will send you Elijah the prophet
before the great and terrible day of the Lord. . . .
And he will turn the hearts of fathers to their children
and the hearts of children to their fathers,
lest I come and smite the land with a curse.

Malachi 3:1-4, 4:1f., 5f., RSV

There are two images of the future in these chapters of Malachi: (1) there is the coming of the Lord to the temple, who will purify his people so they may worship him worthily, and (2) there is the coming of the prophet who will turn the hearts of his people so that the land may not be struck with a curse. Both of these promises are addressed to a sick and divided society. Just what do they say?

Let us begin with the latter promise, the last words in the Old Testament.

Fathers and Sons

For the Jewish people of that time, there was a clear difference between the fathers and the sons. The fathers stood for the generations that had kept the Jewish identity alive through over a century of defeat and exile. Now they were in Palestine rebuilding, only to see their sons attracted to the neighboring cultures and socializing with the Samaritans. The danger was very real that their people might disintegrate, or to use the words of the prophet, "that the land might be struck with a curse."

Something like that is true today. Over two millennia before Freud restated it in modern terms, the prophet saw something about the nature of human conflict and disruption within society, within the family, even within the self. The name "father" identifies not only a social position but a mentality. The father is identified, to himself as well as to others, with things as they are, with order. When that order is threatened, he is threatened. He defends himself by defending it. To do so he uses the tools he has—power, control, authority.

The label "son" also points to a mentality. To be sure who he is, he must prove to himself and to others his independence, since he too equates the father with the prevailing order of things. Any critique of that order is a feather in his cap. Any attack on it gratifies him. Any changes are for the better. He uses the tools he has—insult, doubt, disobedience.

Thus, between the "fathers" and the "sons" the issues are defined: the old order versus change, control versus freedom. Both agree that this is the problem.

And both are wrong.

The way both of them see the tension keeps them from seeing it straight. The power is really not on the fathers' side, for they know the future is beyond them. Their rigid control is an expression of fear, not of strength. Nor is the innovation, the creativity, solidly on the side of the sons. Most rebellion, after all, is sterile and unimaginative. It simply reverses what went before. Rather than inventing, the sons often merely invert; they start with what is and try to turn it on its head. So the fathers and the sons are alike in their reciprocal opposition: both are fearful; each sees the other as strong; each is unaware of the barrier that his own power creates. And because they cannot trust, cannot confidently collaborate, cannot smoothly appropriate in one generation the best insight of the one before, the land is going to suffer.

In the age of Malachi, the "curse on the land" probably meant grasshoppers or drought. We share a world view that makes it hard to see a causal link between grasshoppers and the generation gap. But at the same time the world scope of our culture makes it very possible to see that our air and our water are under a curse because one generation has used nature with no thought for the next. Thus even the image of the curse on the land makes sense again today. When our oxygen has all been replaced by carbon dioxide and our water all saturated with toxins and detergents, we don't have a home planet to return to as our astronauts do when they have run out of reserves.

The One Who Is Coming

Now to this situation the prophet speaks. Another prophet—he calls him "Elijah"—will come. He will heal the rift and ward off the curse. He will not negotiate a new compromise. He will not impose himself. He will not control everyone's responses, but he will, it says, "turn their hearts." He will "convert" both fathers and sons. Into the conflict will come a new mood, a new attitude—not a new law nor a new contract, but a new openness, a community.

Now, certainly, the distance between youth and age is not the only tension in our society. The "generation gap" theme is easily overdone; yet many of the other issues are like it and overlap with it. And if there is no healing, a society can literally fall apart. If the forces of conservation and innovation cannot be reconciled, a civilization can be torn in two, each fragment reacting defensively and fearfully to the other with no room for trust or creativity, no new way out, unless there be come "turning" of the ways.

The prophet does not say the differences will go away. The

sons will remain sons with their urge to invert, and the fathers will remain fathers with their hunger to revert. But the hostility will be healed by that "conversion." But how?

Neither does the prophet say the debate will end. Not that God or Elijah will show the fathers how right the sons were (or the other way around), nor for that matter that God will take a correct stance somewhere between. Something new will happen instead. But what?

For part of an answer we may turn to the other part of the text, the other image—the Lord coming to his temple. Instead of arbitrating among the Israelites, he will judge them. He will purify them. This purity is meant very concretely, for the passage goes on to identify divorce and mixed marriage, fraud and perjury, economic exploitation, and failure to tithe, as the sins that stand between God and his people. First, this must be burnt away by the refiner's fire, so that persons may again be with God—so that they may worthily worship.

Jesus may well have had this same image in mind when, as Matthew and Luke tell it, he was being tempted by Satan, who invited him to make a miraculous surprising appearance in the temple. He likely had it in mind as well when, not many months later, he led his march on the capital and the crowd followed him down the Pennsylvania Avenue of that time and that city, and right into the temple.

For centuries, Christians have thought of that Palm Sunday parade to the temple as a ceremonial religious event. At the most they have recognized that, at the beginning of Passion Week, Jesus had a degree of popular support. But now, after a generation of marches, sit-ins, teach-ins, and even preach-ins, we may have a better notion of the public offense caused by Jesus' action—how it could, as it did, offend both Romans and Jews and lead to his death. Jesus was inaugurating a new kind of mobilization to end the war dividing the human race. Their term for that was "king of the Jews."

Jesus showed us something about ending wars that most of our contemporaries haven't learned yet. Some of our well-intentioned friends think that a war can be turned off like a water faucet—all you need is to get near the handle and be honest. Others think it helps to reverse the roles—to proclaim that the Viet Cong or the Black Panthers, the Sandinistas or the Palestinians, are the good guys, and Washington the bad ones. Such reversal of roles may have some point, but it doesn't end the war. The only way to end the war is to make peace, and for that someone has to die. Someone has to back down. Someone has to be humiliated. Someone has to come up with an alternative, a vision of a new order for which one is ready to sacrifice one's future, one's popularity and even one's life.

Jesus did what Malachi had predicted. He cleaned out the temple. He interfered with the pursuits of people who were making a legitimate living doing business with the temple clients. He brought to bear on their behavior a new judgment which people had to conform to—or leave.

The Other Way

We saw before that the young rebel is often not very creative. The rebel is conformist in reacting quasi-automatically against what the elders do. And usually the rebel is also conformist in reacting in the way others do. We might have argued as well that the threatened "father" is often defensive about things that aren't worth saving or things that cannot be saved by defensiveness. Jesus goes beyond the fearfulness and the self-righteousness of both by bringing into the scene a new option, a new standard, a new demand. He is more critical of the present "system" than mere youthful revolt can ever be, because he has an alternative and not just a negation. Over against the old order he sees a new order—what he calls a "kingdom," the God kingdom—a new relationship where power is used not to defend nor to attack but to serve, an order not of dependence nor of independence but of interdependence. He comes neither to preserve nor to destroy, but to create.

The people who accept this new order will be purified. Instead of hoarding money, they will share it. Instead of being self-centered, they will live for values beyond themselves. Instead of antagonism, they will work for communication.

It is this new order that Christians are committed to seeking and living. But we don't do it all that naturally. For it ever to happen there has to be a change, a "turning," a conversion. Jesus said his hearers, in order to follow him, would have to "repent." Now repentance is not sorrow; it is a change. Repentance is not a bad feeling; it is a new behavior that flows from a new attitude. It is because he demands this change of all, "fathers" and "sons," that he can bring all classes and kinds of people together. The breach will not be healed by toleration, nor by communication (which some think is all we need), nor by negotiation. Healing must be a new beginning.

Whatever you think of particular political issues, you will agree with me as we read the papers that one of the reasons for the state of our society today is the inability or the refusal of persons in public life to say, "I was wrong." There is much talk of new beginnings but little acceptance of blame for the past. We respect the courage and honesty of an individual who is, as we call it, "big enough to apologize," to admit responsibility for past wrongs, and to take initiative to correct them. Why, then, is it so unthinkable for a statesman, or an administration, or a society to do the same?

If we had to admit, for instance, that it was necessary to withdraw American soldiers from Vietnam in 1975, or from Beirut in 1983, why can it not be admitted that it was wrong to send them there in the first place? Why can the statesman not afford to advocate peace without saying it must be "with honor"? Whatever that phrase means, at least, it does not sound like repentance. Why must the willingness to end the war be dulled or perhaps even denied by the demand that we must still seem to have won it? Is it not because persons have closed themselves off from the grace of repentance?

If repentance is the shadow side of the new beginning, its face is reconciliation. Persons can be reconciled to God and enabled to turn to each other, not because God overlooks their past, pride, and guilt, or brushes it off or thinks nothing of it, but because he takes it upon himself—because he himself pays the cost of restored relationships.

The way we've been preached at in the past, "to be converted" sounds like a negative thing. It means a turning away, a forsaking, a turning from fun and frivolity or from guilt and aimlessness, or from bad company. And that's not all wrong. Any right decision, any personal growth, any education does include some rejection of the inadequate, the unworthy, and the false.

But the call of this promised Elijah is not of that shape. This is the turning of the heart toward one another. Any tone of renunciation there might be is drowned out in the reconciliation. The death of self is unnoticed in the light of the rebirth of community. So we don't simply ask, "Who was right?" and "Who was wrong?" nor even, "Wherein was who right?" and "To what extent was who wrong?" We just let go and begin again.

The "Sons" Are Wrong

What is needed is not for the young to have their way. The acculturating thrust toward conformity which to them seems to hold such self-evident attractiveness, because it is different, and because they see it from the fresh side, will turn out to be hollow at the core. It, too, is oppressive. It, too, depends upon unthinking conformity. It is less personal and less caring than the tight-knit minority group, and next year when you need it, it might not be there anymore.

Once you could join a crowd to march to end the war. Without ending the war, the crowd has moved on. If you want a crowd a few months later to march with, it will have to be for clean air or zero population growth.

The sons are wrong. It is only with a heritage that one can be human. It is only in the heritage of Abraham and Moses that a genuinely liberating new order can be brought into human affairs. What the sons need is for their hearts to be turned, for them to come to see the core of the fathers' commitment not as an alien, crushing, senseless assemblage of rules and rituals, but as a covenant they can freely make their own as the very form of freedom—this is what Abraham and Moses were all about. The meaning of *Torah,* of "law"—the meaning of the covenant proffered to anyone who will forsake all who receive it—is liberation.

The long-range purpose of God for Jewish culture was not that it should be swallowed up in the larger stream either of Mesopotamian or of Hellenistic culture, but rather that the opposite should happen. He intended that Jewishness should be opened up precisely by the young Jew, Jesus, and his first acculturated Hellenistic disciples like the young Jew, Paul, to receive the Gentiles. This is, in a broader sense, the meaning of education, as it is the meaning of mission—the discovery of a future direction by way of breaking open the past and remaking it as one's very own future. The only future there can be is the prolongation of the past we choose.

Often the self-styled revolutionaries who deny this are the ones who prove it the most clearly. During the heyday of the "youth culture" of the early 1970s, the noisiest language was that of the disciples of Herbert Marcuse, an old man whose ideas are even older. And if young patriots were to counter the Marxist rhetoric of Marcuse by arguing for red-blooded, healthy-minded loyalty to American values, they generally did it by quoting another aged Californian, Eric Hoffer.

The call to the sons is, then, "Turn!" Be freed from adolescent reaction enough to be able to give your father's concern a fair hearing. Maybe, if the vision of the new order Jesus began has grabbed your loyalty, you can listen to him without fearing for your independence.

The "Fathers" Are Wrong

But that is only half of the prophet's call. What is needed is not for the old to have their way, either. The defensive backward-looking concern which seems to them to be so self-evidently reassuring is a cultural dead end.

However familiar such phrases as "old-fashioned revival" or "back to the Bible," may sound, there is no such thing. An old-fashioned revival is a contradiction in terms. You can't get to the Bible by going backwards.

By the time of Zechariah and Malachi, the mother tongue of the Bible, Hebrew, was already becoming a dead language. No amount of devotion poured out in synagogue schools and ritual could retain it as more than that, except for the professional rabbi. The Hebrew Bible was written in the midst of an effort to take the faith of an Abraham or a Moses and make it the culture religion of a given piece of land, a given state, and that effort had failed. It failed externally in successive collisions with Assyria, then Babylon, then Alexander, and then Rome. It was failing as well internally, in the hardening of the hearts of the fathers toward the sons.

You cannot get to Abraham by going back. Abraham's entire life was one of leaving security behind and going forward to a promise. That is the very meaning of faith or faithfulness. Jesus himself, the letter to the Hebrews tells us, is our model and the one who attained faithfulness. He endured shame and accepted the cross "for the sake of the joy that was set before him."

You can't get to Moses either by going back. Moses was looking forward, away from Egypt into the desert, off the banks into the bed of the sea, away from Sinai into the desert again. He was looking ahead to a land he would never get to enter, looking ahead to an age (which Joshua was not going to find across the Jordan either) when all God's people would serve him as royal priests and all God's people would prophesy. The fathers will not be saved by more careful reading of history, nor by more skilled advocacy of the values of tradition, nor by more effective control of the school. But what if there was something to turn the hearts of fathers to their sons?

If there is one thing we have learned in the struggles of the last decades, it should be that one cannot *preserve* a heritage, if that heritage be one that is devoted to the praise of God and the following of Jesus. The very fences which are meant to defend the heritage stifle it.

Only if the grain of wheat dies will its fertility be renewed in its offspring. Only when it springs forth in a new creative synthesis, where the past has proven the power to take the present up into itself and be renewed, can the past survive at all.

So the call to the fathers is the same: Turn! Let yourselves be freed to welcome as your younger brothers and sisters those who refuse any longer to be your children. Let them, perhaps for the first time, share your values because of their own free choice. Freeing them to make that choice their own might even sharpen your own commitment, if it makes you less anxious about holding before them an unblemished image. It might even enable you to join in that coming great turning which the ancestors called *Amazing Grace*, which the sons and daughters call *The Revolution*, and which Jesus called *God's kingdom*.

It Just Could Be . . .

We won't heal a split society by sawing off the other half. We won't stop protests by asking people to lower their voices, nor will we improve our neighbor's lot by globally condemning "the system." But it might be that:

—if we began to believe that a new order is needed,

—if we let Jesus' judgment break into the way we do our business and handle our money,

—if we let it be said to us that God loves his enemies and therefore we can afford to love ours,

—if we let it be proclaimed to us that that includes people on the other side who threaten us the most—on both other sides;

—if we believe that it is within God's intentions and his capacity to recreate communication where people will open themselves to be instruments of his love, then it could just happen again that hostile hearts could turn and the curse be warded off.

We said that a turning of the heart is not in the prophet's intent an inward, soft emotion. For him it means a new lifestyle and a new moral commitment. If we were thus to listen and to be changed, then it might happen that mankind might not be destroyed. But is there anyone who wants that repentance? Is there anyone who will pay for that kind of reconciliation?

Is There Anyone Here Who Wants That?

It is customary for commencement speakers to say to the new shipload of graduates that the world is waiting for them to save it. This isn't true, and you know that. It is furthermore customary in church college ceremonies to congratulate ourselves on our mastery of the meaning of Christian culture. But we know better.

But do we maybe know enough to hear in words of our own culture the call of that Elijah who came to turn us around?

You are privileged to have been in a school with the international orientation of Goshen College. You enter into employment or graduate studies with an advantage received from a curriculum and a faculty devoted to breaking through the tribalist reflexes taught us by a monolingual, mononational culture. That's good, and you know that. I could say similar things about the service emphasis, or the voluntary campus church structure, or the personal qualities of some faculty members, or of the course of study you have just completed, and you know that.

But none of those merits were worth the trouble—and some were of positive waste—if they do not now issue in an attack on the world's hostility perimeters, if they do not issue in the fulfillment of the promise of Malachi that, through the breaking into their midst of a new kind of servanthood, the hearts of Chicanos can be turned toward the Anglos and even vice versa, the hearts of the blacks can be turned toward the whites, and even vice versa, that between male and female, between town and college, between fathers and sons, there might be that right about-face of the will, that very particular kind of revolution we call reconciliation, which only God can give and which only we can let happen to us!

Commencement address presented at Goshen College, Goshen, Indiana. April 19, 1970.

John H. Yoder teaches theology at the University of Notre Dame. He served in the overseas postwar relief work of Mennonite Central Committee (MCC), 1949-1957; administered the overseas program of Mennonite Board of Missions, 1959-1965; and taught at Goshen Biblical Seminary, 1965-1984.

Yoder has often represented the Mennonites at interchurch encounters. He is a member of the Prairie Street Mennonite Church, Elkhart, Indiana.

He is author of *The Politics of Jesus* (Eerdmans, 1972), *The Original Revolution* (Herald Press, 1972), *What Would You Do?* (Herald Press, 1983), *When War Is Unjust* (Augsburg, 1984), and *The Priestly Kingdom* (University of Notre Dame Press, 1984).

The Christian Peace Shelf

The Christian Peace Shelf is a selection of Herald Press books and pamphlets devoted to the promotion of Christian peace principles and their applications. The editor (appointed by the Mennonite Central Committee Peace Section) and an inter-Mennonite editorial board represent the historic concern for peace within these constituencies.

For serious study

Durland, William R. *No King but Caesar?* (1975). A Catholic lawyer looks at Christian violence.

Enz, Jacob J. *The Christian and Warfare* (1972). The roots of pacifism in the Old Testament.

Friesen, Duane K. *Christian Peacemaking and International Conflict* (1986). Realistic pacifism in the context of international conflict.

Hershberger, Guy F. *War, Peace, and Nonresistance* (third edition, 1969). A classic comprehensive work on nonresistance in faith and history.

Hornus, Jean-Michel. *It Is Not Lawful for Me to Fight* (1980). Early Christian attitudes toward war, violence, and the state.

Kaufman, Donald D. *What Belongs to Caesar?* (1969). Basic arguments against voluntary payment of war taxes.

Lasserre, Jean. *War and the Gospel* (1962). An analysis of Scriptures related to the ethical problem of war.

Lind, Millard C. *Yahweh Is a Warrior* (1980). The theology of warfare in ancient Israel.

Ramseyer, Robert L. *Mission and the Peace Witness* (1979). Implications of the biblical peace testimony for the evangelizing mission of the church.

Trocmé, André. *Jesus and the Nonviolent Revolution* (1975). The social and political relevance of Jesus.

Yoder, John H. *Nevertheless* (1971). The varieties and shortcomings of Christian pacifism.

_____. *The Original Revolution* (1972). Essays on Christian pacifism.

For easy reading

Beachey, Duane. *Faith in a Nuclear Age* (1983). A Christian response to war.

Drescher, John M. *Why I Am a Conscientious Objector* (1982). A personal summary of basic issues for every Christian facing military involvements.

Eller, Vernard. *War and Peace from Genesis to Revelation* (1981). Explores peace as a consistent theme developing throughout the Old and New Testaments.

Kaufman, Donald D. *The Tax Dilemma: Praying for Peace, Paying for*

War (1978). Biblical, historical, and practical considerations on the war tax issue.

Kraybill, Donald B. *Facing Nuclear War* (1982). A plea for Christian witness.

_____. *The Upside-Down Kingdom* (1978). A study of the synoptic Gospels on affluence, war-making, status-seeking, and religious exclusivism.

Miller, John W. *The Christian Way* (1969). A guide to the Christian life based on the Sermon on the Mount.

Miller, Melissa, and Phil M. Shenk. *The Path of Most Resistance* (1982). Stories of Mennonite conscientious objectors who did not cooperate with the Vietnam draft.

Sider, Ronald J. *Christ and Violence* (1979). A sweeping reappraisal of the church's teaching on violence.

Steiner, Susan Clemmer. *Joining the Army That Sheds No Blood* (1982). The case for biblical pacifism written for teens.

Wenger, J. C. *The Way of Peace* (1977). A brief treatment of Christ's teachings and the way of peace through the centuries.

Yoder, John H. *He Came Preaching Peace* (1985). Bible lectures addressed to persons already involved in the Christian peace movement.

_____. *What Would You Do?* (1983). A serious answer to a standard question.

For children

Bauman, Elizabeth Hershberger. *Coals of Fire* (1954). Stories of people who returned good for evil.

Lenski, Lois, and Clyde Robert Bulla. *Sing for Peace* (1985). Simple hymns on the theme of living with others.

Moore, Ruth Nulton. *Peace Treaty* (1977). A historical novel involving the efforts of Moravian missionary Christian Frederick Post to bring peace to the Ohio Valley in 1758.

Smucker, Barbara Claassen. *Henry's Red Sea* (1955). The dramatic escape of 1,000 Russian Mennonites from Berlin following World War II.